Wager

Wager

Beauty, Suffering,
and Being in the World

Raymond Barfield

CASCADE *Books* · Eugene, Oregon

WAGER
Beauty, Suffering, and Being in the World

Copyright © 2017 Raymond Barfield. All rights reserved. Except for brief quotations in critical publications or reviews, no part of this book may be reproduced in any manner without prior written permission from the publisher. Write: Permissions, Wipf and Stock Publishers, 199 W. 8th Ave., Suite 3, Eugene, OR 97401.

Cascade Books
An Imprint of Wipf and Stock Publishers
199 W. 8th Ave., Suite 3
Eugene, OR 97401

www.wipfandstock.com

PAPERBACK ISBN: 978-1-4982-9209-2
HARDCOVER ISBN: 978-1-4982-9211-5
EBOOK ISBN: 978-1-4982-9210-8

Cataloguing-in-Publication data:

Names: Barfield, Raymond, 1964–
Title: Wager : beauty, suffering, and being in the world / Raymond Barfield.
Description: Eugene, OR : Cascade Books, 2017 | Includes bibliographical references.
Identifiers: ISBN 978-1-4982-9209-2 (paperback) | ISBN 978-1-4982-9211-5 (hardcover) | ISBN 978-1-4982-9210-8 (ebook)
Subjects: LCSH: Faith and reason—Christianity. | Apologetics. | Philosophical theology.
Classification: BT50 .B36 2017 (print) | BT50 .B36 (ebook)

Manufactured in the U.S.A.   MARCH 16, 2017

For Micah

To every person I say, "Do the truth you know, and you shall learn the truth you need to know."

—George MacDonald, *A Dish of Orts*

If you are searching for God, then you have found him.

—Blaise Pascal

Contents

Introduction

*A*ristotle taught his students that heavenly bodies are perfectly spherical. He taught this because he thought, for good reasons, that the heavens are more perfect than the somewhat bumpy earth. Until the end of the sixteenth century, Aristotle's theory about celestial objects prevailed among intellectual leaders. So did his theories about biology, ethics, politics, and almost everything else. Some philosophers say that Aristotle even discovered the most basic idea that things are *things*. But in 1610 Galileo challenged Aristotle's cosmology in a book called *The Sidereal Messenger*. Instead of offering a competing theory about objects in the night sky, he actually described what he *saw* with his new "spyglass." His invention brought the moon so close that it looked as if it were scarcely two terrestrial radii away. With his new power of seeing, Galileo discovered that the moon was far from perfectly spherical. It had mountains that were several miles high. The spyglass also allowed him to see ten times as many stars as anyone before him. He witnessed a part of reality that no one had ever seen, and he did this using only the tools that were available to him in Padua—his mind, his curiosity, the materials at hand to build the spyglass, and openness to surprise. Galileo created an instrument for spying out the universe and changed the way that we experience reality. The world as it is accessible to us is what I will call *the local universe*. As far as I can see, this is our only starting place, no matter what part of reality we wish to explore. But it can grow if we approach it with wonder, humility, and all the ingenuity we can muster. Galileo saw mountains on the moon and ten times as many stars as anyone before him because he built the right kind of instrument, and because he accepted reality as it actually showed up, no matter what the prevailing views of the universe were.

I want to think about how we explore reality and how we learn to see the world ever more clearly using a kind of spyglass. I do not know much about how to explore stars, as wonderful as they are, but I am interested in other realities that we bump up against—realities such as beauty, virtue, love, justice, and goodness. These are the kinds of realities that make up a well-lived life. Exploring them is a philosophical act, and philosophical acts are speculative. When I say that a philosophical act is *speculative*, I mean this as a gesture toward the Latin root of the word—the verb *specere*, to look, and the related noun *specula*, watchtower. Philosophical acts are efforts to see things more clearly. But if we want to look at things like beauty or love, what sort of spyglass should we use?

One answer to this question bears on the central point I want to work toward: our *mindful attention* to our lives, shaped in part by our choices, is our instrument for detecting these parts of reality. If you want to see the moon's mountains you have to have a spyglass equipped with clear lenses that have been shaped in a certain way. Likewise, our attempts to spy out this other part of reality depends on the kind of lives we lead, the choices we make as we shape our lives, and the mindfulness with which we pay attention to our lives. Everything that follows is an elaboration of this idea.

Constructing a life is a philosophical act. Philosophical acts that are shaped by a life, and that shape a life, constitute *philosophical style*. Everyone has a philosophical style. Philosophical style is not primarily about the sentences we create to state ideas, though the way we tell others about our experience is certainly part of it. Philosophical style is fundamentally about the way we live in the world through our bodies, our reason, our imagination, and our virtue. It is about what we love and how we are loved.

Philosophical style, as I am using the notion, is always intimately related to local events in a life. As I write this sentence, I am aware of the obvious fact that writing it requires the history of the universe. There is no computer memory bank big enough to hold the complete record of events that led to the flesh that is my hand, tracing every causal detail from the reality of my fountain pen, ink, and paper, all the way back to the Big Bang. No matter. I still find myself here, wherever "here" is, and I have some questions. To answer my questions, I must begin somewhere. As soon as I begin to reflect on the chain of local events from the Big Bang, through evolution, to the writing of *these words*, I cannot avoid the reality that many of these concrete, local events, especially in the last several million years on Earth, were painfully local. Pain is probably the local event that is least susceptible to abstraction, and it is certainly one of the more severe tests of philosophical style. If we are too eager to move past local reality in order to reach "Truth," we can end up with abstractions that do not illuminate the densely populated tiers of the local universe, just as ideas such as "celestial perfection" once hindered us from learning how to see the beauty of the mountains on the moon.

This is not to say that abstraction is not important in philosophical style. It most certainly is. The concept of abstraction forces us to distinguish between what is local in the sense of locatable, as with my pen; what is local but less locatable, as with my mind; and what cannot be located, as with universals or mathematical objects such as numbers. This is an old conundrum, an uncomfortable oscillation between what is local and what is in no way locatable. In experience we discover the difference between what can be seen, heard, smelled, touched, and tasted, and what can only be thought. I feel the contrast between my local experience of my body—so similar to the bodies of brutes rutting about for anything that can be devoured—and my ethereal longing for something that is difficult to name, something like what Saint Augustine found in his own fleeting but transformative experiences that he called the quality of sweetness. I have ideas about the object, meaning, and direction of my longing, but the ideas always fall short. Nonetheless, this experience of sweetness is the fulcrum upon which much of my own discovery of meaning in life pivots and finds leverage. The experience may point toward nothing in the end, but this possibility is part of what motivates the philosophical act. We can respond to our longing like Platonists, relegating the real to a heavenly elsewhere and viewing the local universe as a mere shadow, or we can respond like ontological naturalists and say that longing for more is an illusion, better cured than followed.[1] Or

1. Naturalism can be divided into two kinds: methodological naturalism and ontological naturalism. Methodological naturalism is the foundation of the approach the natural sciences take to studying the physical world. Because these sciences are studying the physical world, and because the instruments and techniques employed in such study are fitting only for the exploration of the physical world, methodological naturalism posits no nonphysical reality, nor does it deny nonphysical reality: it is indifferent to the question of nonphysical reality because it is neither inclined nor equipped to ask questions about such matters. Ontological naturalism, on the other hand, asserts that in the totality of what is real there is nothing more than the physical world as it is accessible to the methods of science. Insofar as ontological naturalists base their conclusion on the findings of the natural sciences, the position is absurd: given that the instruments and techniques of the natural sciences are only capable of exploring physical reality, they can never give evidence that there is nothing more to reality than the physical objects. Insofar as ontological naturalism is a metaphysical position, it must be argued for in terms, not

we can reject both of these positions as too partial. Whatever our response is, the world shows up in its complexity and our responses will always remain uncertain. Pascal said that there is enough darkness for those who do not believe, and enough light for those who do. In this, at least, he seems right.

We ask questions from the vantage point of the commitment central to our lives, our work, and our thought. My own central commitment is closest to a Thomist view of Christianity. But in the sense that some nontheist philosophers are described as friendly nontheists because of their humility in the face of the strangeness of our universe, I would describe myself as a friendly theist. My experience of living fully in the world is both animated and limited by my own committed search—what I am calling philosophical style. Commitment to any philosophical style will lead to ideas, interpretations of experience, and ways of seeing that might be incomprehensible within other philosophical styles. For example, I think it is illuminating to say that the existence of God lends a glow and glory to the universe that is inaccessible to the methods of the natural sciences, a radiance that thrills me. Though my perspective is partial and fallible, the dam does not have to break for me to suspect that the water seeping through a crack is from the ten million gallons on the other side. To me, this kind of lens in my spyglass is clarifying, and it helps me see things in ways that I would not otherwise experience. But this makes no sense at all from within the philosophical style of, say, an ontological naturalist. When I want to talk about the most important things in the world as I see it, I use language that is strange, or even complete nonsense, in the world of an ontological naturalist.

Language is an important part of philosophical style, because it allows us to share discoveries, even if our words always fall short of actual experience. But language does not need to be strange to talk about the strangeness of my existence or the strangeness of my impending death. Language does not have to be strange to talk about my nagging sense that I am not the kind of creature who is better off dead. I play with my children, contemplate God, look at the stars, and enjoy the pleasures available to me by virtue of the fact that I have a body. The fact that I will die, and my awareness of this fact, leaves me full of wonder, among other things. Because I am a Christian, I do not believe that death is the *end* of the story as a whole, nor the end of *my* story in particular, but I do not live my Christian life

---

of the natural sciences, but of philosophy, with all assumptions made explicit. Blurring these distinctions leads to a great deal of confused thought.

with the kind of certainty that the philosopher René Descartes taught us to desire. Philosophy is the act that follows from my uncertainty, along with my desire to see, to understand, and to know. The philosopher's primary tool is the question because questions reveal the contours of uncertainty and the directions for further exploration. Uncertainty is a corollary to all faith, whether theistic or nontheistic, and in our uncertainty our questions can take many forms.

Some questions are more clarifying than others. Consider death. We can ask, "What is lost if I come to an end at my death?" That question helps me see more clearly what is at stake as I approach the uncanny threshold. We can also ask, "What if, when I die, I do not come to an end?" Either I come to an end or I do not, and these mutually exclusive possibilities are deeply relevant to how I view the rest of my life. Even if we are at peace with death as "natural" (whatever that means), most of us eventually come to a place where these questions are important to us. Indeed, for many of us the pain of blank uncertainty that sometimes looms between the poles of these two possibilities is the fire at the heart of our search for meaning in between our mysterious arrival on this earth and our mysterious departure. However we answer these questions about death, our answers will affect the way we think about our experiences of beauty, suffering, and being in the world.

Why beauty, suffering, and being in the world? I use these as place-holders for everything that populates lived experience. Suffering relentlessly pulls on the loose threads of beauty's tapestry. This is one of the ways that I am jarred awake to being in the world. Waves of suffering break on the rock of beauty's outlandish "ta-da" in the middle of a world full of agony. Beauty breaks on the rock of pain. Suffering makes me question the character of the world in which I live. The world is anything but bland when beauty thrusts shards through sheets of raw suffering. We pay attention when suffering shows up on the doorstep of a girl's nearly grown beauty that needs only a little more time to come to fullness, time that will not be given. No world is philosophically boring when it contains so much suffering that we are tempted to say that beauty's terrible draw is an illusion. No world is easy when it includes the beauty of the face of a long-suffering child. We want to rage against the injustice of this suffering, as though there *ought* to be justice in the universe, as though there *might* be. But as soon as we cry out that things *ought* to be a certain way, we feel a profound paradox that keeps our judgment from being too quick, too simple, too final. Beauty lends a "maybe so" to suffering, and suffering a "maybe not" to beauty. In *this* uncertain world of friend and foe *I am. I am*—not in some trial run, but in the only run I have, with each day traded for something whether I wish to trade or not. Beauty, suffering, and being in the world: that is palette enough for the questions I want to explore.

What do I mean by the phrase "the local universe"? There is the universe as it is, and the universe as we experience it as human beings. Whether or not the two universes coincide is an important philosophical question, and we hope that through exploration the two universes will come ever closer together. But no matter how far our spyglass reaches, our experience occurs here, on earth, within us. Our experiences of the farthest stars, precisely because they are *our* experiences, are local. And all the stories we tell are about this local universe. What else could they be about? Everything inside experience and thought happens here in the local universe, and so far, this version of the world is the best I've got.

Sometimes I stand on the ocean shore at night, looking up, and I long to know our purpose. I believe it is possible that we have one. But the implications of the time it took for the starlight to reach my eyes are not lost on me. This is our question: why do I feel like I *mean* something in the universe, even though I know that it took several million light years for the starlight to reach my eyes, only to be extinguished on the cones of my retina, signaling "starlight" to my visual cortex, inexplicably yielding not only the brief recognition of "starlight" in my mind, but also provoking longing, gratefulness, and dread all at once in a creature roughly half a century old? Stars are very far away, but my experience of starlight is very close. I experience what is local, and I merely know what is far away. Stargazing is an ancient and persistent example of encountering a beauty that can lead to dread as easily as it leads to wonder and longing. As I stand in this gap between beauty and suffering, I learn most about being in the world. So we will start there. We will need a different kind of spyglass than Galileo required. If we move toward any philosophical conclusion, it will not come in the form of a proposition. It will come in the form of a choice about how to actually live our lives.

Philosophy is fundamentally the ability to see the world, increasing our awareness of reality in a way that depends on our commitments. These commitments, in turn, depend upon the capacity of our imaginations, the ability of our minds to reach past what we take as "already known" within our lived experience. Our willingness to commit, our ability to imagine, and our openness to new ways of seeing comprise philosophical style.

Philosophy is not something to be sequestered in the university or, far worse, in the professional conference. The philosophical act should not be seen as the purview of a few "experts" because it is constitutive of what it means to try to live the best life possible. Of course, if we are interested in the *best* life, we have to ask the question, what gives something value? This leads us to the moral question, how ought we to act? This raises the epistemological question, how do we know? And so forth. In this way, the entire philosophical world opens up as a result of paying attention to our lives. The challenge is the inevitable *uncertainty* we have about the way we understand and experience the world, along with our inevitable *certainty* about the fact that we must die, even though we do not know when. Despite these challenges, we must commit. My life must follow some path, so even refusing to commit *is* to commit. Not committing is an act of committing to a particular philosophical style that frames a life. There are many different philosophical styles, and one way to learn about them is to look at the historical record of philosophy. Etienne Gilson thought of this historical record as philosophy's laboratory. My brief sketches of various philosophical styles are only meant to be suggestive as we move toward how we embrace a philosophical style in an uncertain universe. But the aim of the sketches is to help us understand what is at stake when we actually wager in this life that is so full of beauty, so full of suffering, and so full of questions.

one

Philosophical Style in the Local Universe

What if Stars Make Music?

Aristotle believed that a kind of music erupts in the wake of the stars as they travel through the heavens. I think that is a lovely idea, but we do not believe it anymore. This simple point is important: the idea was once taken to be true, but it is no longer believed. The point is important because the same thing can be said about any of our current beliefs—one day we might stop believing. For example, one day we might stop believing that there is no connection between music and the movement of the stars. The meaning of music and its connection to reality might not involve a singular pitch, and it might not depend on having enough celestial wind to produce a recordable sonorous swish. But what if music is a kind of wordless order that draws the mind and heart toward something real that cannot be duplicated by a nonmusical source? One of the world's greatest evolutionary biologists, Simon Conway Morris, once suggested that the music of humans, the music of whales, and the music of birds might point to a deeper music that grounds them all, a *universal music*. What if there is a connection between music, harmony, and the order of the natural world? Would this suggest a contemporary version of Aristotle's music of the spheres? What if minds and the sense of hearing require refinement and practice to be capable of fully distinguishing a musical reality from a nonmusical reality? What if this practice requires some level of faith in the prospect that there is music to be heard, and that there are lessons to be learned that only music can teach?

This idea appeals to me, but not because it is provable or somehow useful for astrophysics. It appeals to me because it resists the assumption that meaningful knowledge of the stars, and of nature in general, is limited to material composition—unless the word *composition* is taken to mean something close to "musical." When the stars went silent, we lost a connection between our knowledge of nature, our longing, and our joy. We lost a connection that made our *knowledge* matter because it made *matter* matter. Children look at the night sky and say, "I want to go there." If we ask, "Why?" the only answer that makes sense is, "I just do." They are not merely interested in seeing variations on the rocks that they find in their back yards. This is not to say anything at all against rocks. Understanding the physical composition of different parts of the universe is one of the greatest intellectual adventures in our history. But a child's desire to go to the moon, the planets, or the stars is not the same as the desire to clarify the ratio of helium to hydrogen on another celestial body. Something else draws us to the night sky. The Greek idea of "the music of the spheres" is as good a placeholder as any for what we hope to find or hear out there. Many astronomers share this intangible lure. May the beauty of that nebulous music never be silenced for these explorers. Whatever led Aristotle to choose music as part of his celestial theory might lead us to discover theories that are not so far removed from the wonder of the Greeks.

Aristotle speculated about the music of the spheres, but his goal was to understand the universe, and his theory, like any theory, had gaps that needed to be filled. One gap-filler was the idea of "quintessence." Quintessence—the "fifth element"—was first described by Plato in the *Timaeus* as the element that the Demiurge used to delineate the universe. Aristotle referred to it as ether (from which we get the word *ethereal*). He described it as an element that had no qualities and that was not subject to change. It moved in circles. Quintessence was a useful and curious idea that had explanatory value. This ancient theory was not simply a matter of seeing stars as made of, or embedded in, a peculiar kind of stuff, no more than you would think that the physical composition of the ink you are looking at now is the same thing as what is being said with the ink. Even if the theory seems strange, we can still ask whether or not there is something about the stars that we can read in a meaningful way, perhaps through analogy or metaphor, the art of seeing in *this*, *that*.

If that seems absurd, is it because the Greek intuition about what the stars reveal is absurd, or is it because we have forgotten how to look at stars?

How do we know? Greek philosophers looked at the night sky and decided that the stars were divine beings motivated by love, whose movements made music. Maybe the theory is ridiculous from the perspective of astronomy. But the ways that children (my younger self included) respond to the night sky makes me think that the Greeks might have glimpsed something about the stars that is real, even though it is not testable by physics or geology. Or they might have glimpsed something about the stars as we see them, which is to see something about the local universe—the universe as it shows up on the surface, densely populated with forms. No matter what wonderful discoveries the sciences make, a deep question remains: Why would anyone ever think that the stars are divine in the first place? The appeal of the theory of divinity may have had less to do with explaining facts about the stars than giving an account of our ability to respond to the universe rationally, aesthetically, and with wonder. What does that ability suggest about the kind of universe in which we live and the kind of creatures we are? The distant universe is populated with ice, fire, gas, and very large rocks, but the response of the ancients to the night sky suggests something interesting about what we might hope for in our universe. This is the difference between the composition of a thing and the meaning of a thing.

Among the ancients, composition and meaning were not clearly separated, to the detriment of their science. The theory that the stars are divine beings opens up wonderful worlds of philosophical thought, but it makes for terrible astrophysics if your goal is to fly a rocket to the moon and beyond. The same thing is true today. Composition and meaning are often not separated, but now it is to the detriment of our philosophy, because meaning is often reduced to nothing more than what we discover through naturalistic methods of inquiry into the material world. The naturalistic reduction of questions of meaning to questions of material composition ignores what ancient lovers of wisdom learned from the marvelous experience of living in a world in which, to see the gods, one only needed to look up at the clear night sky.

If the stars evoke the idea of music, perhaps there is something else in the universe besides matter, even something divine. But to say that there might be something divine leaves us with very little detail about the universe. Aristotle thought that there was a complete lack of personal interest on the part of divine reality. The divine reality had nothing like personhood. The pure and constant way that the divine caused the spheres to move in a perfect circle was an idea with a crystalline purity thrilling to a mind wandering among mutable mortals, degeneration, and decay. Dissatisfaction with the material world is not a result of ingratitude or spiritual parsimony, rejecting the bounty of fruits, flowers, or forests available for our delight. But frail and mortal flesh is caught in a wondrous strain between the flux of Heraclitus and the One of Parmenides. The truth of the universe *seems* to demand more than what flesh can conjure, and we marvel that the minds of fleshy creatures can register such insight into the world. To assert that stars make music is just to say that the universe is not mute. Such an intuition does not have to change even if we send probes to actual stars and discover that the music of the universe is not obviously detectable by our instruments measuring the composition of those spheres.

The universe of Plato and Aristotle required a stability that only divinity can provide, not only to get the world going and to anchor identity within the world's continual change, but also to help us understand our own peculiar tether to the universe. If there is something like a world-soul or divine ether, if there is some fifth element beyond the subluminary elements of earth, water, air, and fire, then the divine yearnings and powers revealed through our acts of philosophical contemplation do not leave us merely stranded as an anomaly in a material world. This brief glance at the theories of Plato and Aristotle is only meant as an example of what it looks like for a mind to try to grasp *meaning* in such a strange universe.

Our task, as short-lived mortals, is to circle quickly back to the philosophical endeavor that is finding *our own* way through this world during our short time as we tumble from the darkness of birth to the darkness of death. This is the work of finding a philosophical style, the work of contemplating the world and who we are in the world, the work of spying out the truth. Plato and Aristotle showed us some of the forms of thought that can arise in the living activity of asking fundamental questions. Philosophical artifacts such as the works of the philosophers can express and evoke experience, and they can even make us aware of unseen things that bump up against us and disturb our world. We get inklings of such unseen things in the thrill of the uncanny, and in the joy that erupts when we find hints on the path toward the highest object of human longing, whatever that may be. Our search for this object fills our philosophical coffers with concepts such as beauty, love, justice, wonder, and the good. Some people experience the shocking hunch that not only are we searching for this object, but it is searching for us. The rich history of philosophy is filled with books that carry a reader from proposition to proposition, and the effort to crack the meanings embedded in the sentences of the philosophers is worthwhile. But our movement toward a true wager is an experiment in philosophical style, not as a genre, but as a way of living that includes acts of seeing, imagining, understanding, and responding in thought and feeling.

Back to our question: Why do so many people look up at the stars and find themselves *compelled* to rush back to tent, temple, or tavern, to take up pen and ink, and to face down the white sheet, translating their longings into philosophical propositions or poems so that others can share the experience? That is no more inevitable than Galileo's compulsion to devise a new spyglass that helps us see the mountains on the moon. Galileo could have done something else. He had to work to create the conditions needed for seeing. He had to work to create the right kind of spyglass. The ability to see meaning in the voluptuous beauty of the universe likewise has certain necessary conditions. It requires a life lived in an active, particular, concrete way, *with* and *through* and *as* a philosophical style to which we are committed. By committing, we learn to see new parts of reality, or else we discover that our style is inadequate for taking in the whole and needs to be reshaped. Of course, we might also conclude that there is nothing to see, but then we are left with the question of whether or not this leaves us in the same position as Galileo's contemporaries who insisted that celestial spheres are smooth. Adventures merit risk. Pythagoras was able to encounter the totality of what *is*, and call it a "Cosmos," because he *saw* that order and beauty are rooted in harmony. He *saw* that opposites fit together in the whole through the principle of the logos. In the *Timaeus*, Plato was able to *see* through his myth that there is an intrinsic relationship between proportion, goodness, and beauty. The myth helped him *see* that the cosmos holds together like a living being. And he resorted to music as a way of accounting for the harmony we sense. The form of the idea changes the things that we are able to see. Plato encountered the local universe and came away urgently compelled to write what he saw through a myth, the *Timaeus*. That is philosophical style.

The same can be said for Aristotle, though he was not inclined to write myths or stories. He was interested in concrete realities such as the number of teeth in the mouths of men compared with the mouths of women. He was interested in the genitals of insects and different types of civic constitution. But when he turned to the cosmos, his deepest insight was not about the motions of the spheres: from the perspective of astronomy, the motion of the spheres explains the actual movements of stars as well as Aristotle's dental theories explain why women have fewer teeth than men. Rather, he *saw* something that made him conclude that these heavenly spheres must be arranged in harmonic ratios, with each sphere producing a musical tone so that the revolution of the various spheres in concert produces music in the heavens that reverberates through the world. When we sing or take up the lyre, we accompany the music of the spheres. We participate in the very harmony of the universe. Though he surely meant his theory as a physical theory that said something true about the actual course of the stars, his theory also suggests a metaphysical insight into our universe. The idea of the divine nature of the stars might point to something true, even if the physical details are not correct. Imagine, for example, a first divine act of creation bringing time, space, and energy into existence, and supporting them so that as stars form, and as the universe expands, there is a kind of background music along the way in the form of radiation, a hum of sorts that we can hear with the right instruments. Here once more is the central question: Why did it make sense that the stars would generate music on their way as they move forward compelled by love of the highest divine reality? At this point the question seems more important than the answer. The question keeps the journey from aborting early in a fit of literalism. This capacity to *see* grows from philosophical style. Seeing in turn shapes philosophical style. Even when the details of the reality that we are dimly grasping turn out not to be "true" in the way we thought they were, the universe is still illuminated in a new way.

This portrait of the stars, this flavor of philosophical style, requires at least the possibility of an eternal domain that makes immortality possible for the soul of Socrates, or that deepens grief in the mind of Aristotle, who thought that death likely annihilates a person in whom the divine spark has grown. Such myths are not experienced as *mere* stories from inside this kind of philosophical style because it is rooted in the habit of openness to divine reality. Myths are *true* stories in this richer sense, though the philosopher also listens for the unspeakable substance of the spoken myth, illuminating and enlivening universal truths through stories inextricably bound to the particular. The mythic world is complete and one, with everything named and everything in its place. No event—from the swaying of trees to the clap of thunder, from the birth of a king to the stillbirth of the king's progeny—occurs without some meaning connected to all other meanings, and indeed to meaning itself. Within this world lament can occur, wracking itself against the pillar of the baffling questions about why such loss occurs.

But in such a world, dense with meaning, someone like Socrates can also gleefully unearth the unearthly, letting his mind fly away from particulars in the muck toward pure, eternal form. Socrates asked questions. What is Justice? What is Beauty? What is the Good? He expected these questions to move him and his friends closer to truth. The sense that there is more to the story compelled him toward the fundamental act of philosophy—asking questions from inside the stories we are given, motivated by our longing for and love of wisdom.

"What then is the Good? And what is the best way to approach an answer to the question?"

"The Good? Never thought about it. What's the best way to answer such a question?"

"There are best ways?"

This is how consciousness grows through philosophical speculation. Socrates plied the question to pry minds away from assumptions that halted their growth. But he did so because he sensed that there was truth toward which a mind can meaningfully move.

As the mind awakens it finds rivers of questions flowing between familiar banks. The banks are habits of *seeing*, habits that can only be grown from inside our myths. But the river of questions is the very content of the mythic world melting in on itself, now no longer static but rather in motion. Philosophy is the *act* of a growing consciousness wearing at the banks, changing them. This evolving consciousness, this transformation of the firmament of myth into the flux of Socratic dialectic, is an awakening that is at once joyful, because of the new adventure in truth it presents, and frightening, because of its tendency to disorient through the diminishment of stories and encounters on earth, and through the fast-flowing motion of mind from the stasis of myth to the stasis of eternal verity. This river is a confluence of two rivers: the river Styx (consciousness of death) and the river Lethe (consciousness of our quickly fading grasp on what once seemed certain to us). No wonder, then, that we locate fixity in the forms or the stars while we cope with being pulled toward the divine at the same time that we delve into the aches and cravings that emanate from our material bodies roaming a material land.

How do we meet the world? We meet the world through sense, emotion, imagination, and thought. We assimilate all that appears at the dense surface, in whatever manner it appears. But we also feel compelled to reach past appearance toward something, we know not what. The way the mind is

How do we meet the world?

formed determines what it is capable of receiving. We die, but the stars sing. There is comfort in the promise that something is stable and eternal. We experience the richness of life as well as its transience, and our minds grow in the tension between these two, lending urgency to the philosophical acts in life. In one version of an image that recurs in stories, a bird flutters in at the far end of the king's palace from out of the dark winter, flies over the festive table and past the roaring fire, and then disappears again into a dark and snowy sky, leaving behind a sense of portent. Such is our life. We want to remain in that house of bounty, to remain in that place that feels—and here I mean the word precisely—so *homey*. But our life is bounded by the twin mysteries of birth and death. In between those, for the short time we are on this earth, a philosophical style capable of seeing the stars as divine, and of singing them along their way, is well worth our continued contemplative response as we try to answer the question, what is a truly good life?

What if Stars Show Forth the Glory of God?

In a universe ordered toward a disinterested divinity, the divinity exercises a nonpersonal attentiveness to the only thing worthy of divine contemplation—itself. Marvelous things may emanate from that divine act, things such as Platonic or Plotinian forms, minds, souls, and, far below the god in the hierarchy of being, the barrage of pine trees, birds, and seashells that delight us in our human meanderings, things that are of no interest to the divine mind itself. The divine in the worlds of Plato and Plotinus can be loved, and minds are fired by wonder at the idea that the stars are windows into the world of the gods. In Aristotle's universe, only a dullard would fail to be enthralled by the way our minds break forth in the world of matter, minds that are themselves sparks of the divine reality that is alone worthy of its own attention, that divine point infinitely turned in upon itself, provoking joy in us because of the uncanny circumstance that our highest good also lies in contemplation of that singular Mind.

Being alive and conscious is very different in a universe where the stars are not distant-though-beautiful divinities but are instead *created* beings showing forth the glory of an invisible God, a God who is also responsible for our ability to respond in joyful gratitude and to create hymns of praise for a creation dense with expressions of God's love. When we gaze upon the divine and suddenly realize that God is gazing back at us, we see the universe in a new way—we see that we do not live in a world full of gods, but rather in a world full of gifts. This new vision transforms the night sky into part of God's creation. But this transformation also makes possible a new kind of dread because of the reality of suffering and mal-*form*-ation, the mysterious shadow creeping from the gifts that show up in our four mundane dimensions where vulnerable creaturely life is lived.

As long as divinity, forms, and eternal objects in fields beyond the stars can be contemplated like quasi-mathematical objects, the experience can be captured in the language of a hierarchy of being with almost no need to account for the things in this world that are imperfect and mutable. Whatever grief, suffering, ugliness, and horror reside in the world, none of it is surprising because it simply follows from the mingling of form with matter, the distance of the world from the philosopher's divine "something." Life in a created universe is quite different. When something moves on the page and you realize it is a venomous spider, when the tree limb falls on the neighbor's child, when the mind grasps not only the stars shining in glory but also the vast darkness that sets them off, and when all of this follows not only from the *distance* of the divine from the local material universe, but also from the creative and sustaining *presence* of the divine, then mere philosophical tolerance of venom, thorns, and the carnivorous appetites of unthinking beasts brings little consolation. Whatever else we may say of the local universe, if it is created it is God's. We are uneasy with the equanimity that Socrates experienced at the end of life as he prepared to let go of his body and dwell in divine reality, for either something is amiss in God's good world, or else something is amiss in God. Neither option offers the solace that Socrates found in contemplation of pure form. We are in the muck, and as far as we can tell the very God whose glory shines forth in the stars has something to do with the persistence of the buboes plaguing the village, the barbarians sacking the town.

A creator is no local city-god, no small-time competition for the king. Nor is a creator a self-contemplating Mind. Providence changes everything. It transforms the meaning of my circumstances, the way I experience beauty and suffering, and the substance of my philosophical style that grows as I find my way. Providence changes everything because everything in creation is either intended, or else it is the unintended consequence of something that is intended. And the source of this intention is not some inaccessible Plotinian One, but rather it comes from a God who in some fundamentally important way is a *person*, since our experience suggests that persons intend things in a way that comets and toads do not. We can only hope that the deepest defining characteristic of such a God is love.

Why love? Suppose, for the sake of argument, that a creator exists who is more like a person than like, say, an equation or a slab of stone. When I consider the most valuable experiences, expressions, and accomplishments for persons-with-minds like us, I cannot find a better candidate than the ever-deepening capacity to love. So, if there is a personlike creator, why would I not attribute to that divine person something like, or better than, the highest thing I find among the persons I meet in the world?

Hence the problem. If we find love at the very heart of the universe, and if by "love" we do not mean an impersonal force set against strife to create a myth of universal balance, but rather love that is analogous to our own urgent and active love of others, the existence of evil and suffering is baffling. It baffles in a way that the Greek tragic poets working out the wiles of fate could not have grasped. But it also lights up natural beauty so that when a lush valley between fog-strewn hills evokes longing, I can join Saint Paul, Saint Augustine, and Saint Thomas in hearing a whisper from the same Spirit who once lingered over the darkness and who comes as a comforter. The saintliness of the saints is continuous with the very source that awakens us to this sacred revelation, and to the possibility of gratefulness for the gift of creation. Even my own temptation to depart from the path of holiness is interpreted in the light of this one God who is love. This takes us back to our central question. When the stars become the glory of a loving God who created them to roof the world in which we live, love, create, and work, but also suffer and die, what kind of philosophical style is shaped by this way of seeing?

One answer that people such as Augustine, Aquinas, and Anselm give is that this philosophical style allows praise and prayer to become fundamental modes of philosophical exploration and philosophical expression. Philosophy has as its basic question, motivating every other question, *what is it all about?* In a world created by a loving God whose glory shines forth in the stars and whose command drums on the wayward heart, calling it to holiness, the question *what is it all about?* cannot be answered by any argument or metaphysics that brackets the God in whom we live and move and have our being. This form of philosophical style is akin to prayer. The search for truth becomes not merely a pursuit of abstract universals, grounds for moral action, or theories of knowledge, beauty, justice, and the good. This form of philosophical style is above all the pursuit of the very *person* of

God, and all that follows from the mind and will and love of God. Death continues to shape philosophical style, but no longer as Socrates' immortality of the soul overcoming terror in the illusory world of shadows, nor as Aristotle's grief for this greatest of losses. Death shapes philosophical style because it has been overcome by love and made a servant of God's purposes. This servant is not passive or weak. It has teeth, and it is a hound that will bare those teeth and growl if the child tries to escape into the darkness unprepared for danger. Yes—wind becomes tornadoes and water drowns, the sun scorches and death demands that we let go of every certainty, every familiar crook of our local universe, including that singular part of the universe I call my body, which I have tended, mended, and fed. But at the heart of this philosophical style is the act of reaching inward and upward through the mysteries of faith, hope, and love. This is why Saint Francis of Assisi was able to write, in the "Canticle of All Creatures," "Praised be you, my Lord, through Brothers Wind and Air . . . Praised be you, my Lord, through Sister Moon and the stars . . . Praised be you, my Lord, through Sir Brother Sun . . . Praised be you, my Lord, through Sister Death."

Such a world is not tame, and the philosophical style that arises in such a world is no stoic, calm-eyed stare. Beatitude teeters in the seeker's heart, treading near the steep drop to darkness that seems all too present. The celestial hierarchy that populates the heavens with angels also reminds us that all manner of spiritual creatures can choose badly and populate the lower lands with demons ravenous for a human soul. If we do write philosophical sentences in such a world, we write them as part of a story, part of a universe that unfolds as a story, not because it is a fiction, but because it has an Author.

Likewise, philosophical investigation is a foray into a world that invites us because its origin is the same as the origin of our own efforts to love, imagine, reason, and create. In such a world, however, the things we encounter in nature and within ourselves are not relegated to the category of mere copies that are dimmed because they are far from the original source and caught up in the muck of matter. They are valued gifts put to service in light of God's purposes. Because we are created beings, we are always on the way, struggling with limitation and evil. We are hopeful not only that we can grow in wisdom and love, but also that we are gifted with the possibility of growing in our knowledge of God. This is why Aquinas wrote, "The intellect which has more of the light of glory will see God the more perfectly; and he will have a fuller participation of the light of glory who has more charity; because where there is the greater charity, there is the more desire; and desire in a certain degree makes the one desiring apt and prepared to receive the object desired. Hence he who possesses the more charity, will see God the more perfectly, and will be the more beatified."[1] These two philosophical sentences hold an idea that carries the mind from desire, to love, to contemplative participation in the light of glory, seeing God ever more fully and growing into ever greater happiness. They include an *expectation* that we act, increasing in love and growing in our ability to see God. These two philosophical sentences carry the mind deeper into reality. That is what the local universe is if the stars show forth the glory of God. This is the local universe lived by one who looks up and sees creation.

If the universe reveals God's glory, what is the highest good for humanity? The answer tends toward contemplation not of abstract entities, but contemplation that becomes a form of prayer. Prayer is an encounter with things and persons that are *in the way*, challenging us to love and to act in love. In such a universe, Leibniz's question—*Why is there something rather than nothing?*—cannot be answered with philosophical sentences only, but must also be answered through lived experience. Part of that lived experience certainly involves sentences written by others on the journey of faith, sentences such as "in the beginning was the Word." These lead to canticles and prayers exploring the illumination of Being itself that comes from the strange sweetness of knowing God. This is how we learn to see the glory of God in creation. For someone who has known God, but who now sees the once-luminescent world as so much leaf-rot, detritus, and repetitive pounding of the waves against a shore made up of the crushed shells of the dead, the experience can be more like dejection and bland emptiness. But even the dejection and blandness is defined against a once-upon-a-time experience of God. Whether we see in the light of God's presence, or else find ourselves trying to remember in the darkness what we saw in the light, we can no longer hear Leibniz's question without conceding the *possibility* of God. We grasp the answer to Leibniz's question in our encounters with all that is real, everything lived in light of our commitment to the creator. We become ever more conscious of our strange circumstance. This drives us to demand of God's good world a more thoroughly and permanently convincing witness to the presence of this unfathomable God in whom our faith desperately waxes and wanes. The theist's philosophy is no comfortable endeavor with pat answers. It is an urgent task that hurls us into the tension

1. Aquinas, *Summa Theologica*, I q12 a6.

of a lived world that is all the more tense for being bound up in the mystery of being created. This is the inward life of one who looks up at the night sky and, in the middle of anxiety, prays a prayer of gratitude for the glory of God revealed through the stars. Prayers of need and longing are one side of a fully human response to this sometimes painful mystery, the other side of which is the wonder of philosophical contemplation. The union of prayer and philosophy is possible only in a created universe. It provides a form of philosophical style that is uniquely fit for worship, while at the same time being capacious enough for the kind of doubt that becomes a different kind of prayer for true vision, a desire for a deeper encounter with God, a love of God unwilling to settle for less than the fullness of God. It demands that we relinquish our idols. It is a love that longs for an eternity to explore the unfathomable. Insofar as doubt is a symptom of the incompleteness of our unsatisfactory grasp of an infinite God, doubt accompanies our longing for immortality. *Only* a philosophy that is also prayer could form sentences in which doubt reveals this about us, and about the world that we receive as a whole.

What if Stars Are Just Flaming Gas Balls?

Cogito ergo sum: I think, therefore I am.

This famous philosophical sentence was only made possible because of the monumental changes in philosophical style wrought through Descartes' revolutionary experiment in doubt and his discovery of the thinking subject as the center of philosophical exploration. It could never have been written in an age when the seeking mind primarily looked *out* toward the reality of the divine stars. It would never fit in a world where the stars reveal the glory of God, as though the stars have purpose, as though they both matter and point to something beyond themselves. Descartes' experiment in doubt is a radical turn inward that accepts only our act of doubting as the one indubitable reality that can be known with certainty. Of course, many have doubted the existence of anything that might be meaningful to humans beyond the physical elements we encounter in the world—earth, water, air, fire. The Cynics, the Stoics, and the Skeptics had no qualms with a pervasive refusal to accept anything beyond this world. Nonetheless, the Stoics said that a local universe that is no more than atoms in the void is still our home, and our scope of belief or disbelief is still a response to the reality of our world. The question *How should we live?* still made thoroughgoing sense for them. The reality of their world still made claims upon them as reflective, mortal human beings who desired to flourish.

Something completely different happens when radical doubt is turned into a method for achieving a new kind of certainty. Nothing outside this inner world—and until the thought experiment is carried out, possibly nothing inside this inner world—can resist the juggernaut of this new form of doubt. Descartes thought the whole world was recoverable if reason attended to clear and distinct ideas after the land was leveled with doubt. But it was only a matter of time before his disciples turned their eyes upon the cleared land and found ways to also doubt the clear and distinct ideas. The doubt of Descartes was like an atomic experiment that seems controllable, according to our calculations, but it is new, and one can never say for sure what the final outcome will be until one tries.

Descartes' innovation is often called a break with authority, and in particular a break with the authority of texts. Perhaps. But this fails to address the reasons that these texts, rather than, say, experimental exploration of the world, were embraced as authoritative. The texts from which Descartes distanced himself did not record the universe as susceptible to measurement. They recorded the universe as experienced by conscious, rational, imaginative creatures that seek out the truth about virtue, the existence of God, the way we know what we know, and our experience of beauty and goodness. In a way, then, the experience of the local universe recorded in these authoritative texts was an affirmation of a reality full of meaning, a proper home in which we fit. Descartes' experiment in doubt left him willing to accept only what is certain, and unfortunately he found certainty only in relation to his doubt. This was a profound sundering of the human mind from the fullness of reality, because everything that matters, everything we most wish to affirm as good, can be doubted in Descartes' new sense of the philosophical act.

As science was transformed in the sixteenth century, and as Descartes' turn to the subject gained influence, this subject became the measure of all things in a radically new way. Prior to Descartes, meaningfulness in the philosophies of even the Cynics and the Skeptics was embedded in the relationship of humans to the universe, making sense of questions about human purposes, human ends, and the good life. Descartes' turn to the subject required a starting point that emptied the stars (and everything else) of meaning. It was a commitment to the idea that we can discover genuine knowledge only by embracing a foundation of certainty that is not located in my *experience* of the truth of the universe in which I participate, nor in my *faith* regarding the discoverability of purpose in the universe, but in the *certainty* of my own *doubt*, a different thing entirely. Commitment to this new form of philosophical style occurred just as science began to view itself as the source of knowledge that is independent of the knower, knowledge that is not dependent upon any particular subject's experience, objective knowledge of the real relations among the things of the natural world that exist whether or not there are beings to know them. When we turn inward in this Cartesian manner, the universe turns cold. The measurable world does not light up with glory because radiance is not quantifiable. Descartes did not worry about this because he was optimistic that he could recover everything using a version of the ontological argument for the existence of God. But almost no one was persuaded by that part of his argument. This left Cartesians with little more than Descartes' doubt. If we cannot accept Descartes' ontological argument for the existence of a good God who will recover the rest of what we have doubted, we cannot rejoin the universe, and we become as empty of purpose as those accidental, purposeless collections of gas we call stars. We look up and we look in, but we find only doubt, even if we long for things to be otherwise. A Cartesian with no slam-dunk proof for God is in a *desperately* skeptical situation. Things did not go as planned.

David Hume brought nuance to this post-Cartesian skepticism. In a few pages that were largely unread in his lifetime, he undermined the possibility of inductive knowledge. In case this achievement does not seem revolutionary, I should say it in a different way: Hume devastated the idea of causality and the foundations of science.

What was his argument? Say that I am watching a game of billiards. I see a green ball roll toward a red ball and touch it. I then see a red ball move. What have I seen? I have seen a green ball roll toward a red ball, I have seen a green ball touch a red ball, and I have seen a red ball move. That is all I have seen. What have I not seen? I have not seen a green ball *cause* a red ball to move. That seems like an odd thing to say until I consider that I have also "seen" butane lighters *cause* lung cancer, since a disproportionate number of people who carry butane lighters develop lung cancer. Bertrand Russell offered another illustration using a chicken that was fed by the farmer every morning. Every morning the sun rose, and soon after the farmer fed the chicken. Sun rose . . . chicken got food. Sun rose . . . chicken got food. Then one Christmas morning the sun rose. A few hours later, Christmas dinner was served.

Hume's point is that we should extend this insight to everything, including the rising of the sun and the orderly progression of seasons. Just because it happened in the past does not mean it will happen in the future. What we call causation is something that we bring to experience after we experience a constant conjunction of events. The sun rises, the farmer feeds. The sun rises, the farmer feeds. The sun rises, the farmer cuts off chicken's head. Inductive knowledge goes far beyond deductive logic, and it goes far beyond what is available to us by observation. Cause and effect are not part of what we observe. We only observe this thing, then this thing, then this thing, etc. Hume says that we *never* see causality, and so have no warrant for asserting causal relationships in the world. This is a big problem for science and for mundane life. It is a problem that has not been settled. But it certainly bothered Immanuel Kant.

Kant saw the implications of Hume's skepticism, and he worked mightily to preserve scientific reason in the empirically real world that Newton described, while still allowing for the kinds of knowledge crowded out by Cartesian skepticism—religious, historical, moral, and aesthetic knowledge. Kant called his central project a "Copernican revolution," arguing that order in the universe—the law-like predictability of the universe governed by the regularity revealed in the work of Newton—holds to the law because of what we bring to the world, but not in the way Hume thought. Whatever the world-in-itself may be, it can only be experienced by us in a way that is determined *a priori* by the structure of our understanding. The structure of our understanding, capable of a strictly ordered form of reception, guarantees the predictability of the empirical world as it is experienced, but it does so at the cost of saying anything about the world beyond experience, the world as it is in itself.

Many ancient Greek philosophers thought that our ability to see the form of a thing was divine. Our minds become identical with the form we encounter in the world. After Descartes' radical turn, and Hume's elaboration of skepticism, Kant found his way to a view of the human mind that has some similarities to the ancient view. His theory about our mind's ability to identify with a form such as causality reveals nothing about the divine and nothing about the world as it is in itself, but it reveals a great deal about us as we experience the world, and as we *must* experience it. The ancients looked up at the dome of the sky and saw the gods glowing through the

holes in the dome. In Kant's theory we are the ones who b
universe and space to the stars, not through any choice of
virtue of the kind of creature we are. In a sense, when we
see something about ourselves. The same is true for our n
is likewise bound up inextricably with what we are. It is n
that Kant claims that wonder is most inspired by the starry sky above me
and the moral law within me.

Whatever transcends experience is inaccessible to us. Whatever a star-in-itself may be, it is not the kind of thing that we can know or experience. We cannot know anything at all about such a thing-in-itself. In a strange way, this means that even if our experience of a star *is* an experience of the star-in-itself, we can never know this to be true. It gets worse because, unfortunately, even our very self (as-it-is-in-itself) is beyond our knowledge. And yet we are compelled to desire such knowledge, and we are susceptible to being deceived by our own reason into thinking that such knowledge is possible. The world as it might be known by God disappears over the horizon of our own possibilities, setting like the receding sun. Darkness grows in a universe that once seemed illuminated by the divine. After the sun sets and the dome of the earth is peeled back revealing the night sky, we look up at the stars and we find only ourselves. But at first we do not find ourselves aghast. We find ourselves at home. Kantian space and time have become the very heart of the lived response to the philosophical charge, "know thyself."

What about our moral, religious, and aesthetic lives? What about our hopes? God, freedom, and immortality do not find even a crack in the world of Kant's *Critique of Pure Reason*, and the mind risks being fractured against the stone wall of contradiction if it reaches that far. Nonetheless, as postulates necessary for praxis, and for a life lived and guided in the human world of choice and act, we are compelled toward the ideas of God, freedom, and immortality with a force as strong as any that lays down limits to the boundaries of pure reason.

Before long, the Kantian world stopped feeling like home. Such metaphysical speculation attempted to overcome the failure of Descartes' ontological argument as a solution to the threat of skepticism arising from his doubt-driven philosophical method. But metaphysics began to look less like competition for a contemplative saint's prayer and more like a tawdry, faded exercise in nonsense. Skepticism grew regarding the objects of inquiry that once led thinkers to develop metaphysical systems of thought, stems that were fired by the idea that through dialectic, contemplation, and the mind's engagement with logic, something real and fundamental about the universe might be revealed. Metaphysical systems tried to reach truth that can only be seen with the mind, but that accounts for our *experience* of the natural world, the religious world, beauty, value, and love. These systems were about the *cosmos*, and about our place in the cosmos as beings capable of speculative inquiry. They filled the place that myth once occupied. Our desire for ethereal realities persisted forcefully, but skepticism about metaphysical realities changed the way this desire was understood and expressed. Myth lingered after the setting of the sun, and for a while it shaped the form of philosophical style. Myth, and the residual feeling of myth, shaped the questions, shaped the hope, and shaped the limit of how we experience the local universe as a whole.

One of the most acute diagnosticians of this persistent lingering was William Dilthey. He called it "the metaphysical mood." He thought the metaphysical systems that followed from this ubiquitous human urge were anarchic and contradictory, but he valued the mood as a source of wonder that manifested itself in an important and special way through poetry. He even thought we can re-experience the longings that led to the cloisters of the monks and to the hymns of Martin Luther without sharing their religious beliefs, because all of it grew out of this irrepressible metaphysical feeling.

Like Dilthey, Friedrich Nietzsche recognized and saw the value of that colossal feeling of connection to God that expressed itself through gothic architecture, Dante's poems, and Michelangelo's artworks. But his diagnosis was different, and he drew very different conclusions about the implications of our new skeptical insights. The feeling is lost. If we are truly cut off from the possibility of the divine, severed from this urge that leads mortals to metaphysics and prayer, then we no longer know what work should be urgent. Far from retaining some contemplative and joyful residuum of order, we are instead thrown into a profound disorientation. When the sun truly sets, what once felt like our life-cord linking us to God seems instead to have its far end dangling in space. The cut cord soon falls back to earth, snaking around our feet, tripping us up as we try to reorient to a local universe where prayer merely echoes, tapers, and is absorbed by the nearest collection of dead matter that it encounters.

Philosophical styles like Nietzsche's are often surprisingly optimistic. Stand up. Shed the cord. Find a new way. The way may be science, poetry, or intoxication of one form or another. No matter. Take joy in your new freedom! If there is nothing at the other end of the cord, then the cord is not a link to the divine. It is only a fetter. So, good riddance. Now that we are bereft of gods to populate the fifth and final act of our tragedy, Nietzsche urges us to turn to comedy. At last there is room for laughter.

But a question eventually dawns on us. How long can this go on? Dilthey thought the metaphysical mood would outlast any changes on the horizon of philosophy. Hegel said that philosophy always buries its undertakers. But for many, the darkness of the universe that follows the setting of the sun, the darkness that first produced an eerie but not unpleasant chill on the skin, eventually becomes the coldness of a universe that is cold indeed. The chill goes to the bone. And yet, we love. We create. We mine this new loneliness, for we cannot do otherwise than to persevere in our questioning. Wonder persists, but it feels more like melancholy curiosity. How strange it is that love, beauty, virtue, art, and consciousness are accompanied by that most uncanny of conscious thoughts, the thought of my own annihilation. How deeply strange that this should all grow up on the back of matter and energy flung from an accidental bang, settling into patterns shaped by mass and gravity and other material curiosities, but all without purpose. How strange it is that matter comes to matter to itself.

What do we do with this reality? What do we do when we look up at the stars and, however beautiful they seem, we decide that in the end nothing is there but gas and light and space, elements that just happen to be in the forms of stars and galaxies? Perhaps modern UFO societies represent one form of residual and tenacious hope in response to an otherwise purposeless universe where, as Nietzsche said, life is just a byproduct of a dead world, one manifestation of the universal stuff, and a rare one at that. If there is no God, perhaps at least there are extraterrestrial life forms, and perhaps life on this planet came about from the work of vastly intelligent extraterrestrial beings. Speculation about such things is intriguing, but there are times when it seems more like the last gasp of longing in the peculiar and lonely human world that has become ever more isolated, relinquishing the illusory meanings of appearances in nature as it shows up for consciousness, and instead putting our faith in the hard reality of the purposeless mechanisms underlying appearances, or else diving into distractions.

There is a new kind of inwardness made possible by computers, video games, and the television, the modern forms of the shadows on the wall in Plato's allegory of the cave. John Locke thought of our inner world as a room, a *camera obscura* in which images were projected from a little hole so that we only experience the world as projected, not the world as the world. His idea is profoundly realized when we primarily meet the world through a screen. This strange inwardness is not directed toward the divine mind imagined by Plotinus. It does not wander in the soul's open court portrayed by Augustine, that central place in the soul where a thrilling hope erupts that the spiritual work of inward movement and upward gaze can yield a glimpse of God, transforming this world and giving a taste of the same beatitude that shines out from icons. Many people no longer have a reason to look up. Many have forgotten how to do so.

We become smaller and smaller. For the first time in history, we can see the universe laid out on a map with its billions of galaxies set against a black background. In red letters beneath an arrow pointing at the dot that is the Milky Way, the words appear, "You are here." Next to this, there is a box with a picture of our galaxy. Inside that box is another box with a picture of our solar system. Inside that is a box with a picture of the sun. Next to the sun is the dot that shows the relative size of the earth compared to the sun. We stare. One obvious conclusion is, "I am tiny." But the question that haunts us is, "Am I also insignificant?" If so, we have to ask, "Why should I care?" The central question of philosophy is no longer about the possibility of God, the nature of virtue, or why there is something rather than nothing. The real question of philosophy is the one Camus asked: Why should I not commit suicide?

Within that kind of universe a variety of philosophical styles can arise. One style has a sort of "no-nonsense" feel about it: Can we not, once and for all, be done with philosophical styles that seem meaningful but that do not connect with any measurable fact in the universe? This kind of style often accompanies enormously effective projects, producing "useful" work that precludes a relapse into our morbid inclination to dwell on meaning, or its lack, in a material world. Philosophical style can also take a pseudo-clinical view of the anxiety that seems to dawn when we see the vastness of space and our own insubstantial presence in this largely empty universe, and the curious fact that often we cannot make ourselves pull the trigger. Maybe it is an evolutionary byproduct. The beam of the philosopher's questions can focus on the gap between the reality of human insignificance and our re-luctance to pull the trigger. The gap can be filled with cowardice, dread, or psychic paralysis as easily as it can be filled with humor, arrogance toward the duped peasants, or a sly cynicism. But the philosopher moves beyond all this and becomes genuinely intrigued by the structures of people's lives as they immerse themselves in their institutional roles, or work to exhaustion, or consume alcohol to the point of numbness, or purchase new pairs of shoes with no convincing account of why the other ten pairs of shoes in the closet are insufficient for whatever purpose shoes fill. I work with a philosopher who is making a lot of money from books arguing that there is no meaning or value or purpose in the universe. The strange thing is that he seems to think that his books are important, and that there are better and worse ways to spend university resources. He also seems to think that his students should not cheat on philosophy exams. This kind of apparent incongruence is philosophically interesting.

Things go much deeper than this. When the shock has worn off, some people retreat to the laboratory, some to the four-star restaurant, and some to the mall. But there lingers one sort of melancholy thinker who knows that, however lost in the cosmos we are, we can still love, we can still care, and we can still value. In fact, we cannot *not* do these things. This evokes one of the deepest questions about the meaning of meaning, a question that stretches from Plato's *Euthyphro* to the attempts by contemporary philosophers to address "the really hard problem of meaning in a material universe." What is that really hard problem? Well, if love, beauty, wonder, and everything else that we value do not *ultimately* mean anything, don't they still have genuine value to us even if they arise in a purposeless universe? Sure, we are astonished that there is anything at all, and sure, we are astonished that there are minds like ours. And sure, we are most astonished that our minds can love and create and value and lament. But this just is reality in the material world. No God is required.

Our universe is overwhelmingly improbable. Physicists tell us that there was a 1 in 1023 chance that the initial stable conditions of our universe would occur, the conditions required for the subsequent increase in entropy that we can measure, making possible a universe with stars capable of producing the carbon that is in turn necessary for life forms such as us. And yet . . . here we are. From the perspective of the universe as a whole, the survival of the human species can have no more meaning than anything else in the universe. The accidental purposeless arrival of our minds is no more meaningful than a cluster of rocks on another planet, the presence of water on planet Gliese 433b, or the black hole nearest our galaxy. Because of this, our sense of meaning and value can have nothing to do with any ultimate "purpose" smuggled in under the guise of the intrinsic value of the survival of a species or, more blatantly, the intrinsic value of the "progress" of a species. After all, progress implies an end toward which the species is progressing. If I cannot give a coherent account of a real goal that we are progressing toward, why would I prefer progress in my pediatric oncology patients over progress in the cancer I am trying to destroy so that a child can live for a while longer?

I can think of at least one reason. Our sense of value and meaning simply *is*, as much as any other reality in the universe, because one important condition is met: only persons can value, and we value only insofar as we are persons. My patients are persons. Cancer is not. Rocks are not. The universe is not. But this points us toward something that is crucial. When persons disappear in an uncreated, accidental, otherwise purposeless universe, then purpose disappears. Purpose and value are utterly dependent on the existence of persons capable of valuing or bestowing purpose. Consider the proposition, *Love is valuable*. Is there any other sentence that is a better candidate for being true? Whatever events led to the existence of love, whatever series of accidents was sufficient for its emergence, now that it is here, its value and its meaning to us is not disputable, aside from an ill-conceived reductionism that denies the existence of persons, the kind of reductionism that rarely occurs outside of philosophy departments.

Love might emerge from a history of merely natural events, along with our apparent freedom (whatever that is), our sense of beauty (whatever that is), and our experience of goodness (whatever that is). Or love, freedom, beauty, and goodness might emerge from the mind of God. Or they all might emerge from some combination of these two. In any case, love emerges—behold, here it is. Whether love is the very glue of the universe, or whether two consciousnesses inexplicably show up and love each other for a single hour before disappearing again in an otherwise lifeless, dark, cold universe devoid of thought, feeling, longing or experience, I know as much as I know anything that love is valuable, love is good. Even if I cannot give a satisfying etiology for value or goodness, I still want to say that no matter what kind of universe we live in, love is good. Love is valuable. Love requires persons, just as purpose does. Only persons have purposes and only persons love. Love *is* only where there are persons.

"Love is good." This is the most radical philosophical sentence that can be uttered in an uncreated accidental universe. As long as there are persons who value it, love is valuable. Love *fits* us. So, here is another question: Is there some larger sense in which love is valuable even when there are no persons to love? Well, what would that even mean? If only persons love, there would be no love about which to ask that question. If there were no persons, where would the value inhere? Or to ask it another way, who would value it if there were no persons? This kind of question is very different from questions about the natural events that had to transpire in our unlikely universe in order for love to be possible.

As long as there are persons who love, questions about the value of love are analogous to Saint Anselm's insight into knowledge of God. Anselm said that God is that than which nothing greater can be thought. If being matters, then among the things that we can think, those that exist are greater than those that do not exist. Once you actually have "that than which nothing greater can be thought" in your mind, you just *see* that whatever, or whoever, corresponds to that idea *must* exist. But it is very difficult to get that idea in your mind—as difficult as getting the idea of *nothing* in your mind. Likewise, whatever confluence of accidental or divine events constitute the preamble to love's first appearance in the conscious *act* of loving, once you understand the act, you just *see* its value. Such acts constitute philosophical style, because philosophical style is about seeing the world in a certain way. The similarity of this act to Anselm's fundamental insight into the necessity of God is this: his argument only works inside a mind that has been formed in such a way that it is open to belief and capable of seeing. As we learn about reality, there is a sense in which we see first through our imaginations. Unless our imaginations grow large enough to accommodate such ideas as genuine possibilities, we may never be able to see some parts of reality. We remain too small. The way our imaginations are shaped matters to philosophical style, to the possible ways we can *see* the world.

Suppose this account of value-among-persons is true in an uncreated, accidental, purposeless universe. How does embracing this philosophical style affect the rest of our imaginative formation and our experience of reality? We bring before our mind, say, the concept of beauty—not beauty as it might be defined in a text on aesthetics, but beauty as we *experience* it, something real that can be meaningfully discussed even if it remains ineffable, just as Anselm meaningfully discussed "that than which nothing greater can be thought" without exhausting the reality of God. Lingering mystery never precludes discussion of an idea. As long as we are fairly sure that we are not talking nonsense, we should keep talking. Otherwise

Thomas' observation that we have not obtained full knowledge of even a single fly will bring our scientific and philosophical conversations to a halt.

So, beauty—I would rather have it than not. Now that I have experienced it, I even want to say that a person *ought* to affirm its value, that it is somehow a genuine mistake to deny the real value of beauty, whatever its origin, just as it is somehow a genuine mistake to deny the real value of love. Beauty, like love, has come to be a real part of our experience, so that at least through human consciousness some part of the universe has become aware of itself as beautiful. However we say it, I know the brute fact that I am conscious of beauty, conscious of beauty as valuable, and conscious of my own conviction that you ought to agree with me about the value of beauty, not merely because I prefer it, but because it is truly valuable. We must have some brute facts (or call them starting points, or axioms, or properly basic truths), and this one seems compelling.

Even in an otherwise purposeless universe, statements of *ought* appear because there are persons, and statements of *truth* appear because there are persons. As our minds fill with these ideas that create real value in a *person's* life—love, virtue, truth, beauty—something else emerges: these concepts all point to something *good* that is intimately related to purpose in a life. Purpose shaped by value reveals goodness. Something that serves a valuable purpose is good. The composition of the person valuing in an accidental universe does not seem important. If everything suddenly switched from "material" to "spiritual" stuff, this would not impact the nature of purpose, goodness, or value. The crucial issue is not the stuff of the universe. The crucial issue is the meaning of meaning. Besides, it is very hard to say exactly what we might mean by "material" stuff given all that we have learned from science in the last century. The composition of a universe or a person does not determine its purpose, its value, nor its goodness.

This raises another question. If the universe had a creator who intended purpose in the universe and who meant for persons to emerge, would this in any way impact our sense of the value of beauty, truth, love, and goodness? At the heart of this question is that deeply strange fact that mind—and not just mind, but mind-as-person—whether it is material, spiritual, both, or neither, has awakened to value in the universe, and awakened to joy in response to this value. We long to know whether or not any of this was intended, and whether or not there is anyone to thank (as with beauty) or to blame (as with suffering). Whatever the answers to these questions are, we want to know how the answers impact our being in the world, an act of being that is often painful, often pervaded with anxiety, and often short.

We also want to know whether the value we experience in love, beauty, and the pursuit of truth ought to be shared by other persons, or whether other persons can have very different purposes that are as legitimate as our own but that merely follow from a different sense of what is valuable—establishing the purity of the Aryan race, for example. If there is no purpose beyond what we just happen to value as persons, in what way do we discriminate among the values and the purposes that different persons hold? How do we say that Hitler's values and purposes are any worse (or better?) than Martin Luther King's values and purposes? If it is true that only persons can value, and if there is no purpose to the universe as a whole because it is accidental, then there is nothing outside individual persons by which to judge the values held by individual persons. If it is true that only persons value, and that purpose inheres only in persons, then unless the universe itself has purpose, meaning, and value, there is no way to discriminate among the purposes of individual persons beyond saying that one person's purposes and values are merely preferred over another person's. I genuinely prefer King's values to Hitler's, but you might just as genuinely prefer Hitler's, and there is little I can say about that except something along the lines of, "Yikes!" Even if we can find a way for value to inhere in institutions created by persons (the law, for example, or the *New York Review of Books*), there is still no arbiter of value among institutions, nor between the institution and myself.

That said, many nontheists want to say that there is more to the story than this, and they try mightily to say how it is so. Other nontheists write to cure us of the residual illusions of purpose, moral truth, and love. For example, Alex Rosenberg has written a refreshingly consistent book called *An Atheist's Guide to Reality: Enjoying Life without Illusions*. He introduces his project in this way:

> Here is a list of some of the questions and their short answers. The rest of this book explains the answers in more detail. Given what we know from the sciences, the answers are all pretty obvious. The interesting thing is to recognize how totally unavoidable they are, provided you place your confidence in science to provide the answers.
>
> *Is there a God?* No.
> *What is the nature of reality?* What physics says it is.
> *What is the purpose of the universe?* There is none.

What is the meaning of life? Ditto.

Why am I here? Just dumb luck.

Does prayer work? Of course not.

Is there a soul? Is it immortal? Are you kidding?

Is there free will? Not a chance!

What happens when we die? Everything pretty much goes on as before, except us.

What is the difference between right and wrong, good and bad? There is no moral difference between them.

Why should I be moral? Because it makes you feel better than being immoral.

Is abortion, euthanasia, suicide, paying taxes, foreign aid, or anything else you don't like forbidden, permissible, or sometimes obligatory? Anything goes.

What is love, and how can I find it? Love is the solution to a strategic interaction problem. Don't look for it; it will find you when you need it.

Does history have any meaning or purpose? It's full of sound and fury, but signifies nothing.

Does the human past have any lessons for our future? Fewer and fewer, if it ever had any to begin with.[2]

Rosenberg asks for a fairly substantial qualification when he says that the answers science provides to the questions are unavoidable, *provided you place your confidence in science to provide the answers.* We might as well say that the answer regarding the truth of the charge that a woman is a witch will be totally unavoidable, *provided that you place your confidence in the inquisition to provide the answers.* But his assessment of the state of things in a non-created, purposeless, accidental universe clears away the deadwood left over from a theistic view of the universe, assuming there is no God (an assumption he embraces with a faith worthy of a saint). After Descartes' experiment in doubt, our concept of what counts as real knowledge is sometimes still framed in terms of a demand for a particular kind of certainty, a demand that leaves us alone with doubt, and nothing more than doubt, unless his argument for the existence of God is successful—and most of his readers do not think it is. This is what is so fascinating about what we seem to know, at least when we are not doing epistemology. In the universe as we actually experience it (what I have been referring to as "the local universe") we can use imagination to change our perspective, to see ourselves as a transient speck in the universe, and then shift our frame so that we view

---

2. Rosenberg, *Atheist's Guide to Reality*, 2–3.

our bodies as a universe built of whole galaxies of subatomic forces and structures and strange quantum entities. But the *local* universe, as it shows up at the surface, is also *lived* as grass beneath my feet, breathlessness after running a hill, a glass of wine, a kiss, distant mountains, the moon, and pleasures or pains felt in my body. The local universe is *lived* through our minds that are able to explore, experiment, tell stories, argue, write poems, pray, hate, believe, woo, rend, make music, and breed dogs with exactly the shape and behavior that will win a prize. We engage thought, imagination, and feeling. From within our *lived* experience we seem to encounter truth, beauty, virtue, justice, love, hope, gratitude, and a sense that our impending death is somehow important, strange, and mysterious.

We do not have Cartesian certainty about any knowledge that relates meaningfully to reality. Because of this, we have to ask, "What are we willing to *risk* in order to make sense of the universe?" The idea of risk is central to philosophical style and to the philosophical acts that follow. No matter how we choose, we risk in our commitments. Nor can we avoid committing. To refuse to commit to a philosophical style, and to a worldview shaped by that style, is to commit to the philosophical style of noncommittal. A philosophical style committed to noncommitment risks being cut off from the forms of knowledge that are inaccessible without commitment—knowing other persons, for example, including the person of God if there is a God.

Another way to frame the challenge of shaping philosophical style is to ask a different question. What if there is a fact about the universe that is so strange that it would never be considered unless it was necessary to make sense of the universe as we experience it? Would we have the courage to embrace it despite its strangeness? There are at least two possible "facts" of this sort. One of these is that stuff emerged from nothing, without life or purpose or intention, and then out of this dead stuff consciousness eventually grew to such an extent that it was able to bend back and become conscious of itself *as* a person, so that, at least in this corner of the universe, the universe awakened to itself and began, of all things, to compose songs of sorrow at the transience of life in a world tending toward destruction, a moving myth of the cosmos finding itself awake to itself, only to realize that it is ultimately powerless to sustain its tiny awakening as it is driven inexorably back toward the shuttered night of matter without awareness. The other possible "strange explanatory fact" is the idea of God as creator, the source of our consciousness of all that we call beauty, truth, goodness, and other persons.

These are two very different universes. Both include our conscious-ness of meaning, but each has its own unique perspective on the meaning of meaning. Either perspective will shape our projects if we genuinely commit to it. The choice to view the universe as non-created is sometimes motivated by a resistance to ad hoc explanations of a "first fact." The argument is that if we posit God as the explanation for the existence of "something rather than nothing," we simply push the question back one step, leaving us with God as the new "fact" requiring explanation. So why not use Ockham's Razor and stop at the Big Bang? It is just as unexplainable as God, and it leaves us with one less entity in our explanatory theory. But this is an unfortunate formulation of the question at hand. It is not merely the existence of "something" rather than "nothing" that we want to explain. We want to explain the existence of the universe as it is, complete with conscious, loving, longing, moral, creative persons, as well as suffering and moral evil. There is much to be said about the effort to give the best explanation for the existence of anything at all, but much of it comes down to one question. If we are trying to choose between two ultimate explanations for the cosmos, which fundamental explanation gives the best account for the universe as we encounter it in our lived experience—a nonpersonal origin from nothing, or a personal origin that exists without beginning?

Here the philosophical screw is turned, for life is very short, it is no trial run. I must choose the projects that will occupy my life against a backdrop about which I cannot be certain. Which story is mine? In neither case am I relying on the indubitable, nor the irrefutable. Indeed, in both cases I am relying on "faith seeking understanding," whether my faith is in a nonpersonal purposeless origin of the universe from nothing or in a creator God. But unless my only project is to wrestle with various conflicting possibilities, then I must choose. Other paths include agnosticism (in which case I may still live "as though" the world is a certain way), or else ignoring the whole question and going shopping (in which case I will be living "as though," but in a particularly pathetic way). For those who value the weight and drama of the human dilemma, however, it is not hubris to choose. It is not hubris to live "as though." Nor is it impossible that in so living, life will deliver up confirmation or disconfirmation, allowing us to reconsider our positions from inside a philosophically committed life.

When I say, then, that my philosophical style is bound inextricably to my identity as a Christian, far from having all questions settled, so that I can sit back in undisturbed blessed assurance, I am plunged into mystery of the sort that cannot appear in an accidental universe where consciousness is the result of completely unguided purposeless forces. In an accidental universe, though value seems to appear to the conscious minds of persons, it makes no sense to ask about the meaning of the whole, for however much something may mean to me in a rich and mature sense, there is no meaning for the whole to have, and mind will soon disappear so that no one is left to long for the whole to have purpose.

Curiosity about the puzzles in the universe can fill a life of roughly eighty years, though it seems to me that it could not fill an eternity in any satisfying way. Curiosity about puzzles is fitting for truly temporary minds, and it is a great source of pleasure. In a purposeless universe such curiosity might function as a corrective for minds that are prone to wander toward hope in a God from whom the universe derives pervasive purpose. In principle every puzzle in a causally determined universe can be figured out because it can all be traced to the same stuff. As Rosenberg says, "What is the nature of reality? *What physics says it is.*" Even in a hierarchical universe with Divine Mind at the top contemplating itself, immutability might lead to the same conclusion as ontological naturalism, with a first mover that functions the same way as the fundamental forces of the natural universe, except that it is pure idea or something like that, with everything traced back in a way that is as orderly as our own tracing of universal history back to the Big Bang, where all of sudden we find ourselves shut out of even the possibility of investigation.

Mystery is different from a puzzle. Mystery is something that wonders at motive, purpose, and intent, and it requires the strangeness of a *person* showing up where we thought we were alone—not a first principle, not a first mover, not a force that merely emanates or forever provides the forms shaping matter, however interesting and beautiful such things might be. Mystery does not yield to objective investigation the way that puzzles, curiosities, and knotty problems do. It arises in the context of our sense that the universe is purposeful and that the defining quality of its purposefulness is more like love than like an equation.

The most basic divisions among philosophical styles derive from the place they give to love and its purpose in the universe. This, more than anything else, determines the shape and content of our philosophical acts in response to the lived universe, the local universe, the universe that is my home. If love arises within the various consciousnesses that accidentally appear for a brief moment from local swirls of elements trailing in the wake of the purely nonintentional event we call the Big Bang, then philosophy rightly turns its eyes to other conscious beings and becomes an activity we do on a sinking ship in the middle of the ocean. It becomes an activity that will soon disappear, and it begins by acknowledging the strangeness of our presence in the first place, and of our transience in the second, while affirming the genuine value of others on the ship despite our transience. This affirmation can ignite an equally temporary gratitude for others, or anger at the circumstance of the other's transience, though neither the gratitude nor the anger has a recipient, a meaningful target. Who would we be angry with or grateful toward?

Love also shapes the philosophical acts of those for whom the *lived* experience of the universe is illuminated by the mystery that love is the central clue to the universe. I know of no other way to put the matter than to say that the greatest divide in philosophical style is between those styles committed to a belief that the universe has no creator and those committed to the belief that the universe does have a creator. Nothing we can do or think will give us the kind of certainty Descartes desired. But everything depends upon fully living one way or the other. Living in this way is a profound philosophical act within which we find the forms of meaning and purpose. The exploration and expression of these forms of meaning and purpose both follow from, and consolidate, our philosophical style. In an uncreated universe, we value what we value. But our philosophical stories about that value and its place within our idea of the whole will be vastly different from the stories told about those same valuable things in a purposefully created universe. The nature of love is at the heart of this difference. In both universes, love is the source, content, and sustenance of value, meaning, and purpose. In one universe love can only be directed laterally, toward other accidental persons. In the other universe, it finds an object of vertical love that is without end. A Christian universe is uniquely strange because the subject of vertical love also chose to become a subject of lateral love. Whichever philosophical story we choose to tell, our style will be grounded most fully by what we say about love.

2

Beauty

Beauty as Idea, Beauty as Form

*T*ry again to deeply imagine the two kinds of universes: one is created and the other is uncreated. In both universes, beauty appears
to consciousness and is valued. Beauty can be contemplated,
whether the thinking mind thinks in a world created by an unfathomable God or thinks in an uncreated world in which the very occurrence of
thought is a vastly improbable accident. But the joyful contemplation of
beauty is different in these two universes. The difference can be illuminated
by returning to the image of a universe that is neither strictly accidental nor
strictly created, a universe oriented toward a divine mindlike entity that is
nothing like a person. Call this a "middle universe."

These middle universes (conceived by philosophers such as Plato, Aristotle, and Plotinus) are not reducible to the mere results of matter clash-
ing together, the flux and decay that lead to the accidental mess of fertility,
misshapen animals, and the miserable dry frailty of old age. No, a middle
universe is *ordered* by its relation to a stability that does not suffer variation.
It does not matter whether the stability inheres in the eternal forms, or in
the divine mind, or higher still in the Plotinian One. I want to use these
images as placeholders, general concepts of the ways the universe might be,
so that we can go on to ask about the nature of beauty in different possible
worlds and to understand the significance of the differences among them.
If there are differences, and if the differences matter to how we live our lives
and how we understand the meaning of our lives, and if our lives are short,

31

then clarity from any source will be welcome even though we can never reach certainty of the sort Descartes desired. What other basis could we possibly have for committing to a view of the world, a sense of how things hang together, a sense of the whole?

The idea of divine order in a middle universe led philosophers to conceive of beauty as pointing toward a higher reality, beyond the particular things that evoke the response, "That is beautiful." In this higher reality, beauty, truth, and goodness are related to each other with a mysterious trinitarian character shining into the lower parts of reality where we dwell among the things in the world. List all the facts and you still do not have truth. List all the goods humanity strives after, and you still do not have the Good. So with beauty. In a middle universe the philosophical act compels us to question the things of this world, but to do so as an affirmation that there is more to be known than what shows up locally at the surface of experience. The philosophical act removes obstructions and sweeps away debris so that reality might appear ever more clearly to the mind of a lover of wisdom. But reality remains a thing beyond the local universe, and appearances are merely that—appearances, images of the real.

Beauty holds extraordinary power in such a universe, for while truth and goodness are surely *known*, beauty uniquely *appears*. Language can become enigmatic because this appealing idea is nonetheless strange: beauty *is* only as truth and goodness *appear*. Or we might say that when truth and goodness *appear*, the form they take is beauty. Beauty *is* the illumination of the content of the world, illumination that shines from within things. Delight in dialectical exchange that moves toward truth can approach ecstasy, and contemplation of the Good is unutterable. But nothing erupts in the world that we actually *see* quite like beauty. On our earth with all its writhing beasts, as the sun sets behind the geometrical wonder of the sheer desert cliff thrusting up from the sand, splayed with reds and blacks, beauty *shows up*. In the middle universe we may begin with a woman's beautiful body—the curve of her lip, the length of her eyelashes, the color of her eyes. Sexual desire does not begin to exhaust the longing evoked by the wondrous beloved. Even as we feel the eternal in her face, we know that it will eventually fade to dignified wrinkles, or else to desperate attempts to rouge waning color back into the cheeks. No matter. All beauty that shows up on the horizon carries us beyond. Beyond what? Beyond everything we call the local universe. But it *shows up inside* the local universe. The local universe is the medium of this persistent beauty.

In a middle universe beauty is no mere residuum. It points beyond itself toward something eternal. This is redemptive for those who feel that there is something more to reality but who cannot find evidence of eternity in the actual flesh of the beloved. It redeems and grounds the strange sense—quite literally "sense"—that something lasting beckons to us in beauty, using as one of its media glands that sweat, skin that sloughs, and hair that sheds. Beauty as form, form as stable, and stability as eternal and divine, helps account for what we see in a handsome young man across the marketplace, the unnamed stranger whose history we do not know. We are suddenly overwhelmed with something ineffable. We experience desire, maybe even desire to ravage the ineffable (or as some have put it, to eff the ineffable). But it does not stop there in the philosopher's middle universe, for desire drives us toward a new kind of awareness. When beauty breaks into the world through the stunning young man by the apple bin, the philosopher craves to know whence this beauty comes, to know what beckons to us as he fills his basket with fruit. What is this urge toward something that never fades? Does anything remain when all the crusted world drops away?

The middle universe can be a joyful place for those with immortal souls, because beauty calls us toward home, calls us to real origins that we can scarcely remember now, origins we often fail to recognize in our pursuit of the false satiation of our longings through, say, serial sexual encounters with these strange beauties popping up everywhere. The philosopher of the immortal soul in a middle universe reminds us that whatever pains and griefs and causes of distress we encounter in the world, we should take heart and not allow ourselves to be distracted. In the same way that the stars show forth the ethereal substance of the divine, local beauties are crevices and cracks in this cave we call a world. They let through slivers of light in exchange for which the well-ordered and wise soul should trade the whole world, including that part of the world called "my body." Let the world have whatever it wants to claim. I do not care. The mystery beckoning from beyond the mutable world is a purging fire, burning in the darkness to rid me of all that can be burned away. Anything that remains is immortal, destined to wander among the eternal forms. This is beauty to a Socrates.

The Aristotles of the middle universe tend to be more mortal. They are quite aware of form in the things we encounter and of perfect mind at the top of reality's hierarchy. For them, contemplation of the divine mind is our highest activity. Contemplation connects us to what is most real in the hierarchy of reality and to what is most divine in us. Beauty enlivens this divine element in us. But Aristotelian philosophers tend to be more sorrowful than Socrates. They are contentedly aware of the divine in their better moments, but they also know that this awareness is only temporary. The flame of divinity in our minds merely allows our brief but glorious awareness of the eternal. Our lives are only long enough for wonder, happiness, and grief to flare as three peaks of a soon-fading fiery consciousness. Beauty is the reminder that there is something eternal in this universe, but it prompts philosophical therapies that pry our eternity-conscious minds away from concern over this thing I call "me." Without such therapies I might be sorely tempted to a heavy grief, because I am so very temporary.

A mortal awakened in a middle universe can grasp beauty's link to the eternal, but from inside an Aristotelian philosophical style, awareness of this eternal beauty is as temporary as consciousness in the deadest of dead material universes. This style resists both Socratic and Christian optimism. The tragic is a strange but fitting companion for beauty, and it can inspire a form of sorrow that intensifies our experience of all that is good in the world and a form of courage that overcomes our numbing fear of loss. The tragic aspect of this style is not motivated by anthropocentric self-importance, as though the tragedy is that the universe will be diminished by my disappearance. The universe and its relation to the highest beauty of the divine mind would not be diminished if my transient participation in consciousness of beauty had never occurred, nor would it be diminished by my consciousness disappearing, except, perhaps, for the brief streak of grief I would leave in the collapsing vacuum among the handful of people in the world who know that I exist, and care. In this middle universe we grieve that our own experience of all the beauty in the universe ends at death. Everything goes, from our contemplation of the divine, which gives us a taste of something eternal, to the entire content of our consciousness densely populated by local beauties. We grieve not because we are important to the universe, but because we love this beautiful world.

Beauty in the middle universe is like an inaccessible maiden, the king's daughter gazed upon by the peasant boy who is utterly lost in longing, and utterly aware that he will live and die while she is ensconced in the castle, surrounded by others like her, despite the absolute joy and fulfillment that would appear in *his* world, if only the royal maiden loved him. Beauty in the middle universe provokes a great *if only*. Beauty appeals, but not because of divine intention directed our way. We feel called, though beauty does not call. We feel pulled by the superfluous excess that beauty-as-such exudes, but beauty does not notice us. Beauty draws us to the lake covered in fog, and to the distant cluster of trees beyond it, and to the hills further yet. The draw is so powerful that we eventually wonder whether it comes from something more than a static eternal form or an emanation from an inward-looking and unchanging divine mind. In the middle universe, we experience a quiet delight as we learn to see how the beauty of the stars connects with what is true, what is good, what is divine.

Our questions go deeper as we try to discover a true way to speak about beauty as form, as eternal, as co-equal with truth and goodness, even as it breaks into the world through the face of a humble young woman distracted by apples in the marketplace. In the throes of seeing her for the first time, I may feel my heart rate rise and my belly churn so that I want to approach her and hide at the same time, but I do not ask questions about beauty's nature yet, for what is the purpose of asking questions when the thing itself is so fully present? But eventually I want to know what it is about her that inspires me so profoundly, what it is that makes her the portal into the idea of eternal beauty. Is it the proportion between her eyes, nose, and lips? Her symmetry? Her order? Perhaps. But Igor in the hayloft has symmetry, including his perfectly midline hump and his two equally proptotic eyes, right?

Whatever we say about order, symmetry, and even radiance, we never get to the deep ontology of beauty without the ineffable, unutterable, eternal form of beauty. Even if the idea of "eternal form" turns out to be incoherent, it is *still* the idea that feels most true about beauty in a middle universe. Something is coming through that feels permanent, unconditioned by time. If the form of beauty exists somewhere in eternity beyond the multitude of local gods, or else in the purity of the divine mind, it does not matter too much if our definitions are somewhat vague. Beauty beckons. It seems alive. And yet we know that artists create beauty in works of art intended for the minds of others. Art does not show up without an artist. Could this be a clue about the universe, with beauty scattered everywhere, cramming crevices and caves, flowing over dunes and seas? As we ask what beauty means, we begin to spy out ways that beauty connects with truth and goodness. But beauty as the beckoning *appearance* of the eternal can provoke the question, who is speaking? That question ought never to be begged. But it certainly should be asked. What if real beauty is not the downward flowing of a static eternal form, but is rather the *expression* of a speaking God?

Beauty as the Glory of God

Saint Paul wrote that star differs from star in glory. If physicists discovered that our familiar universe emanates from a divine mind, this would have a strange, and possibly enlivening, effect on our vision of the world. The effect would be stranger still if the divine mind turned its attention to the other conscious beings in the universe, so that our experience of beauty was not merely a sign of our fleeting participation in an eternally self-contemplating divinity, but was rather a gift from a creator with the capacity to relate to us in love.

If the universe is created, our thoughts and experiences of beauty become radically different than they would be if particular instances of beauty merely emanate from a disinterested, impersonal divine mind. In a created world, beauty is not a mere byproduct. It illuminates the true character of reality. Beauty is not an attractive ornament. It reveals the truth of nature as much as any scientific discovery. In some ways, maybe more so. In a universe that is even possibly created, beauty compels us to open ourselves to the truth about reality, without explaining it away. We must endure mystery, but endurance in a created universe is a joyful adventure because of hope. If the world is created, our insight into beauty can grow because there is always something more to be grasped. Aquinas said that the created nature of things is the bond between being, goodness, and beauty. If he is right, in the same way that being itself does not distinguish the *forms* of things that exist, neither does beauty distinguish these forms. Insofar as a thing *is*, it is beautiful. This means that overcoming the limits of our ability to see the beauty of the things that *are* is a genuine kind of growth that allows us to see creation more truly, to better see glory. Our very seeing becomes an act of prayer and worship. As we mature and grow and comprehend through attention, contemplation, and prayer, the world will answer our questioning minds in the form of beauty until, just as we come to see the being of the cosmos as a whole, we will be able to fully see the beauty of the whole, and finally the goodness of the whole.

When Saint Paul said that in God we live and move and have our being, quoting pagan philosophy to the Athenians, he did so in the context of a brief but powerful characterization of our experience of seeking: our journey often feels like we are groping after God in the darkness, though God is not far from us. Suppose that is true. Even so the experience of beauty reveals something about this intimately present and sustaining God, whether it is the local beauty we find in the flower garden with its path leading into the darkness of the surrounding forest, or the beauty Dante saw in the face of Beatrice who, evoking the thrill of desire, also became a portal into a deeper knowledge of what beatitude might be. But here is a question from inside a created world: What do we do with the beautiful spiderweb transformed by dew in the corner of the garden? What do we do with the web transformed by the morning event of a created, trapped insect having fangs pierce its belly, filling it with venom to digest the inward parts for consumption later in the day? In an intended universe the stars show forth the glory of God. Does the beauty of the dew-covered web do the same? Or is the web a case of beauty gone awry? Robert Frost, in an exquisitely constructed sonnet about a white spider holding a dead white moth, asks what power brought the spider and the moth together: "What but design of darkness to appall?—if design govern in a thing so small."[1]

The spiderweb is the quintessence of beauty with all the metaphorical suggestiveness this implies: it is a fifth element, something besides the chemistry of web materials and the wetness of the dew. Whether or not insects feel pain is a neuro-entomological question. But their struggles to escape the web, and the writhing of their legs and wings before they capitulate to the paralyzing poison in their abdomen, is philosophically disturbing, if indeed design governs in a thing so small. Does Robert Frost's question uncover a potential motive? Should we answer along with him, "What but design of darkness to appall?" If the universe is created, how else, besides malevolent design, does a moth end up as a hollow shell sucked dry and left to crumble after the web is abandoned? Is it better to hope that there is no design? Saint Augustine certainly did not think so.

One who believes the universe is intended can experience natural beauty as noumenal. But is beauty still a source of illumination when the mind's beam lands on the dining spider and the dined-upon white moth? If we set things that are beautiful in nature against things that are horrific, do we gain insight into the creator's mind? Like any text, the book of nature must be interpreted, and we are fallible interpreters. When I see the beauty of the dewy web beside the horror of the spider fangs penetrating the abdomen of a living creature, I bring my own memories of B-grade horror

1. Frost, "Design," lines 13–14.

movies from childhood with a horse-sized spider approaching a lovely girl. Frost's portrayal of the white moth's horrific fate leads him to conclude that either there is no design, or else the designer is not the kind-old-man-in-the-sky we meet in childish images of God. But there are much older images of a complex creator. In the Genesis myth, after Adam and Eve ate the apple (or orange), God's first act was to make them garments of skins. It is not hard to concede that God is stranger than our common images suggest. The question, of course, is whether the strangeness of God is malevolent.

The wild beauty of this universe surely erupts from nothing tame. Intention complicates the picture of both beauty and suffering. Nature's complex and strange beauty is different from the way we might choose to arrange the world for own comfort, safety, and settled sense of the familiar. The universe is a massive stage for beauty. Before Copernicus and Galileo, it was easy to imagine the universe existing *solely* for the shaping of human consciousness. We can no longer imagine that, but it is still an interesting question whether God might make use of this stage, and its awful awe-filled aspects, to shape consciousness. In a created universe, whatever the meaning of beauty, sublimity, horror, existence, and divine activity, when human consciousness shows up on the stage it is not absurd to wonder if our sense of longing beneath the stars, or at the sight of a distant mountain range, is somehow fitting, not in the sense that it is merely appropriate in the face of such beauty, but that it is quite literally the response that best fits the way our minds are meant to encounter beauty in the universe. Such a possibility only makes sense in a created universe, which is to say, a purposeful universe. But if this is true, several other interesting questions arise about beauty, our experience of beauty, and our own creation of beauty.

If we live in a universe created by God, even if the only thing we can say about God is that God *loves*, beauty in nature rightly inspires gratitude and curiosity at what the meaning of beauty is. Beauty reminds us not only of our place in nature, but also of the difference between ourselves and nature, a difference revealed by our conscious witness and evaluation of the alien world of the spider in the spiderweb with the white moth, provoking poetry because we are so moved. Difference does not imply indifference. Whatever we experience as natural beauty existed hundreds, thousands, billions of years before our consciousnesses appeared to encounter it as beautiful. Beauty appears, rising through the stuff of the universe to reach our conscious minds. If this is God's creation, then this just *is* what it looks like for stuff to *appear* from the strange will and mind of God. Beauty is

not dependent upon the beholder in such a universe, nor are all behold-
ers equally capable of seeing this beauty as it is. Whatever is beautiful in
nature is already there, appealing because it emerges from the creative
act. Whatever variations we bring to the event of beauty, the existence of
a creator enlivens the experience of beauty because the circumstances for
the eruption of beauty into the world, though not intended for me alone,
were nonetheless intended. Because I am also a created being, my ability to
experience created beauty is one way of reaching across the chasm between
myself and the rest of the natural world. Beauty is the radiance of a created
thing, and we see beauty as radiance just insofar as we grasp the things
we see *as* created by God. The better we learn to see, the more we see the
beauty of being, until finally the whole world is beautiful, and we come to
understand the power of evil as an enemy of true being. Evil appears as an
absence of beauty, either because a thing's being is diminished through evil,
or else because our ability to see is diminished through sin. But the more
we become the kind of people who can see beauty in this way, the more we
realize that the experience is also suffused with love, reciprocated love.

Whatever the mystery of God may be, my increasing consciousness of
creation's radiance and meaning is an adventure. *Adventure* is a word that
fits our encounter with the riches both of nature and those objects of contemplation such as the idea of nature-appearing-beautiful. Contemplation
of the beautiful is not an exercise in sorting out the details of what beauty
is. It is the spiritual discipline of entering into beauty as one way that the
inexhaustible reality of God is revealed. Beauty expresses God's otherness
even while God reaches toward us. This can be said in many ways, none of
them adequate. These kinds of sentences attempt to shape and clarify the
idea that in a created universe beauty is not prior to God, nor is it a limit of
God, but rather it is an important and fascinating way that God becomes
known through creation. The purpose of such clarification is not to get the
idea right. The purpose is to encourage the deep act of seeing well, since
this living act is the only testing ground for the truth of beauty.

Learning to see is learning to know. This is an interesting and important part of the philosophical exploration of beauty in a created universe.
Nothing is wasted in creation, not even waste, because superfluity itself can
stand as an expression of abundance and a sign of the boundlessness of love
for one whose philosophical style allows that kind of vague but suggestive
way of experiencing the world. Thinking about such distinctions is useful
as long as it does not distract from the lived act of contemplating creation's

beauty, the necessary starting point for thoughtful exploration of beauty. Our understanding of the occasions for our contemplation of beauty is not exhausted by genealogies of our own categories of experience, nor by geological descriptions of events over eons that shape the valley copse and distant mountain. Our capacity to arrive at such thresholds, our ability to show up at the feast, cannot be fully accounted for by our underlying neural structures. The mystery remains.

How does such glory deepen our consciousness of reality? How does beauty's illumination of the universe grow our souls? How does beauty in a created universe enable us to understand God, to worship God, and to love God, each other, and ourselves? This last question—part philosophical, part theological, part psychological—in no way depends upon anthropocentric claims that the universe was created for humanity and that in humanity the universe has reached some pinnacle. We do not know much about celestial hierarchies, if they exist, and the aim of such learning is always the humble aim of knowing more about God and God's good creation. But because a living philosophical style yearns for understanding about reality, in a created universe it is riveting to ask how beauty contributes to the growth of our conscious minds that also reason, love, and pray. Through beauty in a created universe imagination, reason, love, and prayer converge. In a created universe, this convergence is a central aspect of beauty, and of our own creation of beauty.

How so? Minds search for meaning. Even pessimists about the reality of meaning in the world often wish they could find meaning, a wish that suggests something about their meaning-seeking minds. Minds also create meaningful things, such as works of art that appeal to us through beauty. Each of our senses reveals reality in a different way, and so this is not meant to privilege the act of seeing. But if we can grasp what we receive through sight, we might learn something about the meaning of what we encounter in a poem, music, the taste of food, the world of smell, the sound of bird songs, and other kinds of non-seeing activities that open up our experience of beauty.

Some visual art is political, of course, and some is philosophical. Certain political and philosophical ideas are stated best through such art. When Marcel Duchamp signed a urinal with the name "R. Mutt" and named the piece *La Fontaine*, the piece raised a question in aesthetics in a different, and perhaps more interesting, way than, say, a paper on aesthetics asking the question, what is art? Duchamp was an artist, and to some extent

La Fontaine asserts a kind of creative authority and a power of naming. It did not have to tether explicitly to questions of beauty or meaning to be interesting. But when we look at a painting that foregrounds some aspect of nature—foregrounds, say, a darkness that threatens, or a lighted window, or the wateriness of lilies—we recognize something from our own experience of beauty that we might have missed without the painting. The artist's own act of seeing helps us see the world in a new way, and part of what we care about in the painting is that it came from a person's mind.

We enjoy learning to see in a new way, and this act of seeing must be lived. It resists propositional expression. In a created world, because beauty has a kind of reality that would be incoherent in a purposeless world, our response to the beauty that another person has seen and revealed through a painting can be contemplative silence and attentiveness, but also prayer. Why prayer? Because part of the adventure of a created universe is that signs of God's goodness might show up around any corner. When they do show up from any quarter, including art, they are a cause for rejoicing and gratefulness. Joy is response to happiness, and happiness is moving closer to our intended purpose and our proper relation to what is real. If knowing God is our true end, then beauty deepens our happiness, because beauty is one way in which God is known through creation, if only in the sense that without God beauty does not appear in such a universe, for without God nothing appears. Whatever the complexities of evil and suffering, this at least is true: beauty appears, and it astonishes us.

If the appearance of beauty is in some way dependent upon a creating and sustaining God, and if the fullness of beauty's meaning cannot be expressed directly and fully in propositions *about* beauty, then who is to say that minds currently incapable of philosophical, literary, or theological propositions might nonetheless be receptive to *wordless* meaning as it *appears* in beauty, whether it is the beauty of nature, the beauty of a face, or the beauty of a single fly buzzing around in the room? In beauty, meaning resists being distilled or translated from the manner of being we call "appearing." This opens up the prospect that the intellectually challenged who can never read the works of Augustine or Aquinas, and who will never touch the world's great ideas in literature, mathematics, or science, might nonetheless be capable of encountering the meaning and appeal of God through beauty. Regarding such speculation we are given no insight, but the idea is attractive, and even without knowledge, one who hopes in God can hope for this, or trust that there is something even better.

Beauty as Tragic and Redemptive

Beauty emanating from an eternal self-contemplating divine mind fits a universe of stable order and proportion. In a created universe the beauty that erupts through the skies, valleys, mountains, and gardens of our wild and variegated world feels both terrifying and homey, both strange and familiar. But what do we do with beauty that comes neither from a divine mind nor a divine creator, but which nonetheless seems mysterious and uncanny, lighting up all that is most wonderful about the world against the tragic backdrop of our transience? Dwelling in the house of beauty seems like a great answer to the outrageous absurdity of a universe without God.

Nietzsche had a keen sense of this view of beauty within a philosophical style in which God is dead but not forgotten. Nature can produce things that seems horrible to us—misshapen bodies and morally askew monsters. But in the absence of eternal verities or a creator, beauty opens our eyes to nature as the sole reality against which we can measure our own purposes and ends. Natural beauty is astounding without being vacuous, even without a connection to the divine. Beauty can tempt us to see nature *as* a god—a kind of fallen god, not in the sense of morally fallen, but in the sense of falling from the heavens of the ancients and landing here with enough force to suffuse the world with mystery. Beauty becomes an experience of divine presence, without God. Beauty holds the same appeal in such a universe that metaphysics did for Aristotle—in one sense, it is the most useless of things, and yet it is so valuable that all the rest is reasonably traded for some small portion of it.

Within a philosophical style such as Nietzsche's, beauty is the benchmark for every other assessment of value. But such praise can also become a kind of worship that tips into madness. Absorbing the effects of beauty under the influence of nature's shiver and light can make us useless for other things. Suddenly beauty seems redemptive, or tragic, or strangely enough, both. Beauty seems redemptive when it is juxtaposed with everything that is boring, petty, or bad in some knavish way. Nietzsche lauds the capacity of a godless world to erupt in beauty. He wants a godless humanity to overcome terror while creating beauty in the face of the vast darkness and empty silences of a purposeless and mostly dead nature groaning under the façade of our philosophical contrivances. Beauty seems redemptive. But it only *seems* redemptive because, while we retain the language of redemption, we have no coherent notion of redemption. Redeemed from what? Redeemed for the sake of what? There are no real ends for humanity, no real purpose beyond what we ourselves generate. Beauty is only *apparently* redemptive because the sense of redemption derives from the tenacious lingering of God's shadow, long after God is dead. It is only *apparently* redemptive because it does not actually redeem. How could it, if we cannot say what we are redeemed from and what we are moving toward? Salvation from boredom is hardly a robust salvation. Those who experience a more substantial enemy than boredom demand a deeper redemption.

Even after God is dead, God's long shadow can manifest as the aesthetic appreciation of religious expressions in the form of scripture as literature, churches as places of propriety without talk of holiness, or tasteful icons chosen to decorate the living room because they go well with the carpet. Aesthetic trading on this remainder is more seriously philosophical when it links the beautiful with the tragic, but this is no better than empty redemption. The tragedy of such thin redemption is also merely apparent. It is nothing more than the spending of time, or else a waste of time if there is something better to do.

If beauty in such a world can only be *apparently* redemptive, in what way is it only *apparently* tragic? With the residuum of God's shadow hanging over human experience of the world, there is still opportunity to regret the death of God, to feel the absence, to consider the loss with true sorrow. Nietzsche's experience of beauty awakens him to the delusion of those around him who are not so enlightened to the loneliness of the universe, and who continue to misconceive the meaning of beauty through religious art and architecture. Such people fawn over the work of Michelangelo and the builders of the great European cathedrals—beauty of the sort that can only follow upon faith in God, according to Nietzsche. The gratitude of such people to a nonexistent creator is genuine. In the presence of these responses to beauty, the naïve practices of the unenlightened make tragic thinkers acutely aware of their own loss of that hope that there is more to the universe than meets the eye, the loss of a conviction that the part of the universe that meets the eye as *beauty* merits joy and gratefulness because it points past itself, however valuable it may be in its own right.

When the experience of beauty evokes a longing that can only be satisfied by the God in whom we cannot believe, the longing is reframed as high tragedy, but it is only tragedy in relation to the quirk of human desire. It is melancholic, tempered by the shadow of our own transience and the loss of our sense that there might be some eternally real being answering our hope. Longing is juxtaposed with sadness, and the waning light with growing shadows is felt in an aesthetically meaningful way worthy of poetry, art, music, and philosophy. For a while this is sustainable through societies, clubs, and movements. Even churches can perpetuate this approach to beauty, especially when it is accompanied by at least a children's story of a God safely ensconced somewhere out in the universe, a sort of divine Santa story for the kids.

How long is this sustainable? Apparently quite a while in some forms, though even in churches prone to this aesthetic approach the congregations seem to be shrinking. As these institutions thin with time, insight, and forgetfulness, the tragic thinker learns valuable lessons from the crisis uncovered by this approach to beauty. The most valuable lesson is perhaps insight into regret. Sorrow manifests in the presence of beauty not because of the beauty, but because it would have been so wonderful if the longing and the hopes sparked by beauty had some correlate in reality rather than being illusory. This regret can at least make intelligible the otherwise baffling experience of those believers who rejoice in gratitude to God when faced with natural beauty, and who rejoice at the well of mystery and meaning uncovered by great art because of the common divine foundation of the artist and the subject of the art. Regret accompanies the memory of the old idea of harmony, whether this be the harmony that flows from Plotinus' One, or the harmony that follows from the unified sweep of an attentive God's continual act of creation.

Such regret can give one insight into the past. It can demystify otherwise indecipherable motives for holding apparently ungrounded convictions. It can also lead to pity, or else a kind of weary elitism that allows the peasants to have their comfort without the disruptions of philosophical critique, encouraging the calming effect that such feelings seem to have among the masses, one form of anesthetic for temporary consciousnesses quickly flitting through a universe that is on its way to utter silence. Harmony might be a balm, but in such a universe the enlightened mind will find no reason to suppose that the resonance of its own conscious longing with natural beauty is grounded in anything other than a purposeless series of events that might have been otherwise, accidents that might never have yielded the odd flight of this occupied speck we call Earth. The same enlightened mind can wish there was more to beauty. It can ponder the curious fact that when matter became aware of itself and the universe, it so commonly, irresistibly, and strangely began telling stories about God.

These feelings foraging among naturalistic fields for sustenance cannot be sustained. Regret runs its course until we finally relinquish the mood and turn to tasks that fill up one day after another. Some feel relief that we are no longer shackled to desires that can never be fulfilled. Some feel sorrow at the bleak universe that lies beyond the edge of our greenish, warmish, homey patch hurtling through the darkness. This is less of a philosophical conclusion and more of a philosophical cure, removing the cause of the *dis-ease* so that humanity can stop pining after some purpose in the universe, when meaning and purpose are simply not to be found. Once the cured mind passes the last beacon of longing for the unreal, what is beauty then?

The Beautiful as Pleasant but Purposeless

What is the naturalist's consolation in the face of death? There are some simple comforts. Whatever the answers to the great questions are, the end of life is more peaceful if the family's finances are in order, the house is tidy, and there is no unfinished business. When the desk is cleared of all but the most necessary things, and when arrangements are made for relief of suffering should it come, the day can still be punctuated by happiness at the face of a friend, the presence of a pet on the bed, or a few minutes by the window looking at a beloved garden. The idea that death is utterly the end of a conscious person might still seem strange, but baffling questions need not hold power over calmness, for quite literally it is what it is.

If a reprieve suddenly occurs—say, the new medicine the doctor gave for lack of other options turns out to work better than anyone expected— nothing changes about the naturalist's universe, the certainty of death, nor the finality of death. But from that calm perspective on the precipice, no longer prone to questions about the meaning of meaning in a material world, nor to periodic swoons over the tragic beauty of the world destined for naught, there can be a kind of unencumbered appraisal of beauty, a pure act of sorts that stands before beauty as beauty, unconcerned about the mythical behind-the-scenes connections of beauty to the good, the divine, or any other metaphysical fill-in. Beauty may have no more inherent meaning than any rock or chemical reaction, but it is still beautiful to us. From this clean and uncluttered perspective there is *mere beauty*—a sunset at the lake, a flower among weeds, a face in the crowd that smiles and is lost.

Beauty that refers to nothing beyond itself is perhaps best appreciated when we live fully aware of our mortality. Transience shapes our meditative responses to whatever appears to consciousness—now beauty, now the memory of beauty, now the calm persistence of darkness. But even in such a distilled and pure consciousness the question can recur, is the value of beauty something that endures aside from my own experience and feeling? This is a version of the philosopher's conundrum: If a tree falls in the forest and there is no one to hear it, does it make a sound? The question about sound has been answered by the neuroscientists. The answer is *no*. Sound is constructed in our brains from shifting patterns of air, vibrations of membranes, hinging of small bones, and transmission of these events to our brains via the eighth cranial nerve. This does not necessarily mean that everything is constructed by our brains. The tree, whatever a tree is, falls whether we are there or not. But absent ears and brains, there is only air movement, not sound. Is beauty an analogous sort of thing in this kind of naturalistic universe? Does beauty exist only if there is a conscious mind seeing it? If beauty requires consciousness in order to exist, does this change its value? If beauty does not exist apart from consciousness, we might be tempted to some form of emotivism. But even in a naturalistic universe, emotivism is not necessarily the only possible account of beauty.

Here is a thought experiment. Imagine a universe that is simply a disintegrating corpse—all light extinguished, gray on black, dead, cold, with no activity other than large masses hurtling farther and farther apart from each other. Next, imagine a universe in which a sun shines brightly and a planet rotates, creating the appearance of a sunrise over mountains and valleys, with lengthening blues, receding shadows, and newly illuminated forests of pine frosted with last night's snow. Does this second universe have anything of genuine value that the first universe does not have, even if no consciousness exists to experience the beautiful sunrise? My first inclination is to answer yes, but as soon as I do, I find myself smuggling in frames of perspective, a conscious seer-of-sunrises, as a byproduct of imagining. So, what if consciousness of a sunrise is a necessary part of what we call "a beautiful sunrise"? Would this mean that beauty is merely subjective since it is dependent on a subject, or would it mean that beauty is an objective reality that simply requires the physical presence of a perceiving and appreciative consciousness in the same way that it requires the presence of mountains, sunlight, and snow-frosted pines? If beauty is fundamentally what I *experience* as beauty, and if there is no beauty apart from my *experience* of beauty, then it is true that if no consciousness existed there would be no way to claim that a universe *with* beauty is more valuable than a universe *without* beauty. Why? Simply because there could never be a universe without consciousness that nonetheless contained beauty. But this does not necessarily mean that beauty is not objectively real. After all, the sound of a tree falling in the forest requires a hearer in order to exist, but that sound is nonetheless objectively real, if anything is.

This view of the nature and value of beauty is distinct from emotivism because it articulates the objectivity of value by identifying "consciousness-framing-the-beauty" as just one more material ingredient in the natural world. In other words, the event we call "beauty" might be nothing more than a material human consciousness plus the material thing perceived by the material consciousness. If so, beauty is as objective as any other chemical reaction yielding results as tangible as an explosion or a change in the alkalinity of saliva. This objectivity does not mean that every consciousness will experience beauty any more than everyone experiences sound. Because material consciousness is a necessary ingredient, and because no two material consciousnesses are the same, the objective event of beauty may not occur when a different material consciousness is placed in the same environment, any more than the chemical reaction that occurs when I add sodium to a test tube does not occur when I add potassium to a test tube instead. Beauty becomes objective in a naturalist world by being pried away from the ideas of meaning, goodness, and truth. The objectivity of beauty is purchased at the price of making the conscious mind merely one more object. Beauty is as objective as a chemical reaction, and it is just as meaningless.

If this idea is coherent—and I am not sure it is—we can ask another question about the two universes. Is the second universe (with light and color and so forth) more valuable even in the *absence* of the chemical event we call consciousness, simply because it has all the other ingredients necessary for the objective eruption of beauty if a consciousness ever shows up? Again, the idea that sound requires a hearer does not diminish the reality of a well-executed Mozart symphony even though, for the music to show up in the world, the physical events of bow on the string and breath in the flute must also have the physical event of hearing for the musical beauty to erupt in the material universe. Sound has to be experienced by a person to be real in this sense.

The point can be put another way. If beauty exists, and if nothing exists except objective, material, determined entities, then beauty is objective. The same is true of Hitler's assessment of the value of Jews. The event we call "valuing" results from the material conditions we call consciousness. What else could it be? Conscious experience of valuing beauty points to nothing except its own surprising emergence from determined, accidental, natural events. It is just an objective event among objective events. Seen in this way, the value of the second universe might hinge not on the presence of beauty, but rather on the reality of being the kind of universe in which beauty is *potentially* present, should consciousness show up on the scene, just as sound is *potentially* present should a hearer show up on the scene. On this account the difference between the second universe without consciousness and the second universe with consciousness is that when the chemical event we call consciousness is present, there is an object that actualizes beauty the way that an object (the hearer) actualizes sound. However, if there is no consciousness present, the objective chemical reaction we call *value* in the second universe never shows up, just as light never shows up if the material realities necessary for it are only potentially present, but never actually formed into light-emitting things.

So where does the value of that second universe without consciousness show up? One might say that it shows up in *our* universe where there are actual conscious objects capable of thinking about the variety of possible universes. This a very different account of value than the account offered by the emotivist or by the pseudo-platonic naturalist who wants to allow certain structures in the universe to be objectively beautiful without a conscious perceiver. But for a naturalist who wants to retain the objectivity of beauty or value this seems like the kind of account that is needed. Beauty and the event called valuing beauty must be objective events in the sense described by the chemistry of neurotransmitters.

If the neurochemical event of consciousness is necessary for the existence of beauty in a naturalist's universe, and if beauty is objectively valuable in the account just given, how does consciousness realize—make real—this value in such a universe? It is hard to say much more than that the chemistry of consciousness *brings with it* the capacity to value. I realize that it takes a great act of faith to believe that a staggeringly improbable, accidental, purposeless chemical event such as consciousness brings with it a capacity to value. But I do not see any way around it from inside the philosophical style called ontological naturalism. For some *thing* to be valuable in a universe in which there is no meaning or purpose beyond that which is brought into the universe through the chemistry of conscious experience, the thing must be of value to *someone* whose chemistry makes them experience value. In the kind of universe under discussion some philosophers, such as G. E. Moore, have tried to argue that even apart from the existence of the complex chemistry of someone-to-whom-something-matters, there are things that matter. Apart from the existence of anyone in the universe for whom something is valuable, they believe, there are realities such as beauty that are valuable, realities that confer a kind of priority in a hierarchy of "good things" that do not depend on the possibility of the chemical event of valuing. I have difficulty making sense of the idea that value is an objective part of uncreated, accidental existence in the absence of a person capable of valuing. At the same time, if value does inhere in the universe, with or without the chemistry of valuing, that is the kind of thing that we think conscious persons *ought* to embrace, if a consciousness ever begins to exist. When consciousness does show up, presumably the chemical act of valuing can be mistaken so that the "wrong" things are valued or called beautiful, placing the measure of value somewhere besides consciousness. But does it make sense to push the ground of value and beauty and meaning out of consciousness and back into the universe? If the universe is itself purposeless and meaningless, it is not a likely reservoir for value.

This is where the question of the durable value of beauty in such a universe becomes even more interesting. For the sake of argument, say that the ingredients for natural beauty include nature arranged in a certain way and seen as beautiful by a valuing, fully determined, accidental chemical event—the consciousness of a person. Likewise, for artistic beauty, say that the ingredients include the made artifact and the accidental chemical event called "the artist's consciousness" that conceived and created the piece of art. In both cases if there is an *experience* of beauty that is valued by the chemistry of consciousness for, say, five minutes, it does not seem far-fetched to say that such a universe would have even more value in it if beauty were appreciated for ten minutes. Between two entirely accidental, purposeless universes, one in which there is a chemically determined accidental consciousness of beauty for five minutes, and another in which there is a chemically determined accidental consciousness of beauty for ten minutes, I am inclined to say that the latter universe is a better universe. A similar argument might be made regarding two such consciousnesses experiencing beauty for ten minutes, rather than only one experiencing it for ten minutes. Even if the universe reverts back to the same eternal deadness that preceded the brief eruption of these two consciousnesses that became aware of beauty, I would pick the universe with two consciousnesses over the universe with one. Why?

If the consciousness of beauty is valuable in an otherwise accidental, meaningless, purposeless universe, then by extending the duration or number of chemical events that result in such consciousness, the quantity of value in the universe is increased. In this limited sense, the presence of consciousness seems to impact the value of the universe and the value of the circumstance called beauty, whether natural or created. If there were a universe with an *eternal* consciousness capable of experiencing beauty, that universe would be even more valuable, especially if that eternal consciousness were also a creative consciousness capable of adding beautiful things to the universe.

This thought experiment suggests that a universe created by, and valued by, an eternal God is more valuable than one that is uncreated and empty of valuers. But it says nothing about how the existence of God would change the value of *my own* experiences of beauty, truth, goodness, virtue, or whatever other valuable thing we put in the blank. Some aspects of the experience of beauty might be the same across all universes, created or uncreated. If so, then as long as I am capable of valuing the experience of beauty (or joy, or love, or justice, or goodness, or truth), it is objectively true that there is genuine value in our universe, even if the universe as a whole is meaningless. That said, it is still interesting to ask if the intimate relationship of value to the consciousness of persons suggests anything more about this mysterious home of ours.

Go back to the thought experiment with one accidental consciousness in a purposeless universe experiencing beauty for ten minutes. Suppose this single consciousness of beauty in an otherwise meaningless universe suddenly had a second thought in the ninth minute of its ten-minute existence—the thought, say, that it has been preceded by, and will be followed by, an eternity of nonconscious meaningless reality, and that it is not only fleeting but also *alone*. This would probably profoundly change its experience. If it became aware of the impending eternal loss of this great good that it was experiencing—ten minutes of beauty, and its own self-conscious value—its last minute of consciousness of beauty would surely be different than the first nine minutes. It might be horrified and frightened. It might despair. It might become a Stoic. Or it might become a theist, even if theism is just wishful thinking. If it did become such a theist, it might wonder why things are arranged this way.

For the moment I will leave that consciousness hanging in its last minute of existence, because at this point in the thought experiment another important experience is evoked—the experience of dread. We do not live in a world that is just full of beauty. We also live in a world that is full of suffering. Before thinking further about the experience of that single consciousness in its ninth minute, we have to address suffering as it appears in different kinds of universes. Only then can we think about ways of being in a universe that is so obviously filled with beauty and suffering, wagering on a philosophical style when the stakes are so high.

3

Suffering

Suffering on the Stage

*E*veryone suffers. For those who have not yet suffered, be patient, you will. If the idea of beauty is a placeholder for what we value in the experience of our lives, suffering is the counterweight we put in the balance. Wretchedness is not assessed in absolute terms, but rather in the relative terms of what might have been, or perhaps what ought to have been—that my eyes not be blind (so that I can see the world in all its beauty), that my child not die (so that his or her life might come to full flourishing), that my lungs not be filled with cancer (so that I might enjoy the simple pleasure of easy breathing). Suffering that comes from injustice might have been otherwise in a just world. Suffering from starvation might have been avoided by the good of food; suffering from rape by peace, continence, and love on the part of the rapist; suffering from anxiety by whatever it is that answers anxiety, an answer that is itself at the heart of the philosophical endeavor.

We suffer loss, and it might have been otherwise. A remedy for one kind of suffering can lead to other kinds of suffering. We can *think* about suffering using the language of good things that are destroyed, value that is missed, and minds that are torn from contemplation of beauty and forced to witness agonies. But the actual *experience* of suffering is not always cast in those terms, and it may not be cast in any terms at all, for some suffering is beyond the last beacon of language available to us. Whole languages have been rendered mute by great suffering.

Suffering on the tragic stage is not of that sort. On the tragic stage we do not gather as witnesses gather around someone who is in the throes of actual suffering. Though everyone gathered either has suffered or will suffer, we come to the stage for other purposes. On the tragic stage suffering of some sort is *portrayed*—the death of a beloved child or spouse, social ruin, moral abomination. On the stage we portray inadvertent horrors, intentional injustice for the sake of personal gain, the fall of the great or, more poignantly in some cases, the fall of the average person for whom the small amount of good accumulated in a life is lost through some avoidable error, a disproportionate consequence that renders bankrupt a life that will never be repeated.

Why do we gather at the tragic stage? We may show up in the theater just for the spectacle of the thing, either a spectacle of horror or one of sentimentality. Aristotle discussed this motivation in his *Poetics*, and then he discounted it as void of insight into the nature and value of tragedy, though he acknowledged that spectacle will go on because spectacle sells. We may go for a chance to reflect on our own lives, as the suffering represented in dramatic concreteness mirrors the very situations that reveal the meaning and urgency of our short lives. Portrayal of suffering that we have in common with others may help us see something important about ourselves and those around us, or it may shine a light on the solitude that certain kinds of suffering can bring when associated with shame. It may serve as an historical reminder, an opportunity to relive a traumatic experience once we have healed somewhat. Whatever the stage (film, play, book, poem), tragic portrayals often appear after moral horror such as the Holocaust, slavery, or 9/11. We may also go for preemptive moral shaping—if you are thinking about infidelity, *Madame Bovary* or *Fatal Attraction* might make you pause.

Whatever our reasons for gathering at the tragic stage, there is a corollary "stage" that is philosophical. On this stage various forms of suffering are interrogated, probed, and tested to understand what is *yielded* through suffering, both in the sense of being produced and in the sense of being relinquished. Philosophical questions are directed like a spotlight on the impact and meaning of suffering for an individual. Suffering bears on moral responsibility and the shape of a worldview. It can disclose within a single person the presence of virtue and vice, magnanimity and monstrosity. The circle can be drawn larger to include a community (Columbine and the philosophical questions about education of the young), a state (Texas and questions about the death penalty), a nation (Tuskegee and questions about the rights of human beings in a research trial), the world (pollution and questions about ecological ethics), the universe (Voyager space probe and questions about how to portray Earth and its inhabitants), and the supernatural world (how can there be a good God in the face of so much suffering?). The philosopher is the actor on this stage. Sometimes the act is scripted and sometimes it feels more like improvisation. But not all suffering can be reached in this way, because some suffering is so disruptive and unutterable that there is scarcely an observing "I" remaining—there is only suffering. Perhaps it can be reached by a philosophical mime, if there are such people.

Questions on the philosophical stage are different than questions on the tragic stage. The tragic stage portrays suffering. The philosophical stage draws conclusions. It draws conclusions in the sense of deriving, but also in the sense of sketching out meaning or its lack in a way that fits the memory or the anticipation of suffering. This drawing is a process both of discovery and of creation. It is discovery in the sense that its questions mine something found in the world, something we come up against that will not yield and that pushes back against us. It is creation because it involves our fallible attempts to shape a philosophical style that fits the reality of suffering without flinching in the face of truth, neither shying away from hope where hope is possible nor losing nerve when truth seems closer to our fears. The philosophical stage, insofar as it is a stage, strives to be public. As it strives to be public, one means by which it becomes public is through the philosophical sentence, in the same way that poetic experience is made public through the poetic line, and the tragic stage is made public through the expressions, gestures, interactions, or absence of actors.

Absence can play an important role in the public character of suffering, whether it is the absence of God in *Waiting for Godot*, the absence of intact language in the brokenness of Paul Celan's poetry, or the absences of coherent egos among the tortured in Elaine Scary's *The Body in Pain*. Ruin is often best portrayed and considered in relation to what is absent. What is absent on the stage might be hope, thwarted and unfulfilled, or else something of great value (or small value made great in bleak contexts) that is lost.

One of the oldest examples on the philosophical stage that illuminates the reality of death—the one reality that threatens loss of everything, including the experience of suffering—is the contrast between Socrates on his deathbed and Aristotle talking about death in the academy. Aristotle's language developed exclusively on the philosophical stage, made up of lectures, notes, and texts. But Socrates played out his own philosophical act of dying on the tragic stage, portrayed by Plato in the form of dramatic dialogue, even though he rejected the "tragic" character of death. These two accounts uncover a fundamental division in philosophical postures toward death. In both cases there is some sense that life must be lived in light of the certainty of death. Philosophy is preparation for death. There is a clarity of value provided by death when it is viewed through the lenses of different philosophical styles.

Socrates was at peace and nearly jovial as death approached. He thought that he was embarking on a great adventure, and that his weeping friends were being ridiculous. Something wonderful awaited him. Death is a threshold. Once he passed beyond it, he would fully encounter a reality that appears only as a shadow in this life. Death is the fruition of everything the philosopher pursues, and it is the only way to move beyond the apparent suffering in this imperfect shadow-world that is so prone to error and decay. Death is the portal into the realm that fulfills our longings. So stop grieving about something that merely *appears* to be loss. When this body finally drops away, you are free, and all the philosophical activity of a well-lived life is revealed at last for what it truly is, namely, preparation not only for the courage needed to face the moment of death, but preparation for unveiling philosophy's central discovery. Whatever it is that strikes the heart to joy in this journey toward wisdom is also the very thing we meet on the other side of death. This is why Socrates harshly criticized the poets for their portrayal of suffering, ill fortune, and tragic death on the stage. Their plays lied about suffering and death. Philosophical preparation for the hope Socrates found in death orders the place of wealth, virtue, and love in our lives.

When Aristotle stepped onto the philosophical stage, immortality was most definitely not a settled point. If any part of us does survive death, this is no reason to look forward to it. Even if the divine part of me that allows my own highest activity in contemplation turns out to survive the death of my body, that does not mean that anything I experience as "myself" will see the other side. There is no "other side" for humans since the soul is not something separable from the body. For Aristotle, death meant the loss of everything.

On both the tragic stage and the philosophical stage the stakes are high. We want to flourish, but death approaches inexorably, compelling us to avoid delays in our search for what human flourishing is. We have no choice but to trade this day for something—far better that it be traded for a day of flourishing than for a day of behavior that diminishes or degrades us. If the tragic stage helps us see what human flourishing and human folly are, then let us have our tragedy. The looming reality of death means time is short. We need all the help we can get.

We want to make sense of suffering and death. Socrates, Plato, and Aristotle thought that philosophy could teach us the meaning of death. But for those who think there is no meaning to discover, "making" sense is "making it up." If it is true that when we are dead we are gone, we should just live life as it approaches, enjoy it as we can, and if suffering strikes, take comfort in the fact that it will be temporary. This is still a way of living in relation to death, but only in the sense that the idea of impending annihilation can help us avoid the distractions that accompany false hopes for life after death. Sometimes we suffer, sometimes not. But neither the presence nor the absence of suffering changes our place in the universe. It is what it is—get over it, and get on with it. This approach is very different from that of Socrates, Plato, and Aristotle. It is also far from the world portrayed in Ecclesiastes where the sun rises and the sun also sets, because in that kind of world the writer's teeth are set on edge as he leans into the wind, accepting that this is just how the world is, but with a tenacious sense of how *good* it would be if things were otherwise, a sense he will not relinquish even though it causes him pain.

Suffering on the tragic stage or the philosophical stage tends to be a human-sized portrayal of suffering—Socrates on the deathbed, Aristotle in the lecture hall, Epicurus in the garden. If gods are anywhere to be found in this portrayal it is of little consequence for local events. Virtue in the face of suffering fosters human solidarity in the pursuit of a well-lived life. Suffering on the stage is characterized by the hope that our understanding will be deepened as we explore the meaning of human suffering. This will prepare us for our own suffering and death in a way that matters at the purely human level, whatever the gods may think. However, if there is a creator of the universe, something important changes. A creator carries responsibility for the possibility of suffering, even if the universe is structured so that suffering is redeemable in some way. Unlike suffering on the stage, where the lens is on the nature of human suffering, in a created world the lens turns toward God and our relationship to God. The meaning will not be found in any event bracketed from the truth of the whole. The meaning of suffering will always relate to the person and presence of God. What does that universe look like?

Suffering in a Created Universe

The existence of God changes our experience of suffering as much as it changes our experience of beauty. Gratitude is the placeholder for the thoughts, feelings, and actions that beauty evokes. Is there or is there not someone to *thank*? Suffering raises a different question. Is there is or is there not someone to *blame*? If the universe is accidental and purposeless, or if it is populated by distant, self-absorbed gods, suffering is still suffering, but it is not inflicted or maliciously permitted, even if, in the middle of agony, our cry takes the form of "*Why?*" However, if there is a God responsible for the universe, and sufficiently involved in it to make sense of prayer, the experience of suffering is very different. As they say, now it is personal. Everything that was uniquely attractive about beauty in a universe created by God is reassessed in light of suffering. We wonder whether the gains are worth the price. Framed in this way the questions seem intractable, but not because of a lack of philosophically sophisticated arguments about suffering in general. They seem intractable because of what we feel when we see the face of someone who is actually suffering. Can a created universe make room for *this* and still be called good? Gratitude for beauty makes no sense in an accidental universe, nor does the complaint that things are not as they ought to be. If there is no God, philosophical questions about reasons for suffering disappear. But introduce a creator who is not merely a first mover, and suddenly our distress has an infinite target, for the greater the power available to a person to make things otherwise, the greater the fury that they are not so.

More than most experiences that we have, suffering lays bare the differences among philosophical styles. If I go to the doctor complaining about a sharp pain running down my right leg, I am suffering and I welcome a solution. But the pain just is what it is. However, if the doctor discovers that I have secretly been drugged, and that someone placed a small device under my skin that sends pain down my leg every time she presses a button, my experience of the pain changes dramatically. The pain was merely pain until I discovered that another person was responsible. Rage in the face of suffering is analogous. Mundane life might seem to be the same whether or not there is a God, but suffering makes the question urgent, because either God causes our suffering, or else God permits it even though it could be stopped. All other things being equal, anger seems not only understandable, but perhaps even obligatory, if there is no other way to understand it. "I will tolerate pain even if I do not like it. But you permit my pain, or even cause it? And for no good *reason* that I can see? How dare you!"

Here is another response to suffering in a created universe: "I am convinced that neither death, nor life, nor angels, nor rulers, nor things present, nor things to come, nor powers, nor height, nor depth, nor anything else in all creation, will be able to separate us from the love of God in Christ Jesus our Lord."[1] Or again: "Even though our outer nature is wasting away, our inner nature is being renewed day by day. For this slight momentary affliction is preparing us for an eternal weight of glory beyond all measure, because we look not at what can be seen but at what cannot be seen; for what can be seen is temporary, but what cannot be seen is eternal."[2] The Apostle Paul's "slight momentary affliction" included injustice, imprisonment, hunger, flogging, snakebite, and shipwreck. In the universe as Paul understood it, the words "slight" and "momentary" are not meant to understate the suffering in the world, suffering such as that endured in, say, crucifixion. Paul does not bracket the intensity of our suffering. The philosophical style expressed in his sentences cannot be understood apart from the meaning of "love" in the first statement, and the meaning of the phrase "eternal weight of glory" in the second.

Saint Paul is not doing theodicy, trying to get God off the hook. He is contemplating the unimaginably improbable enigma of the universe and our experience of it. Saint Paul's universe must be seen as a whole to make sense of it. Otherwise his response to suffering will be misunderstood. In *The Brothers Karamazov*, Dostoevsky dramatized this misunderstanding in the exchanges between the monk Alyosha and his brother Ivan. Ivan clipped stories of horror from the newspapers, and he showed them to his brother. In one of the stories a servant boy had accidentally hurt a dog with a stone. The landowner set the other dogs on him, ripping the child apart before his mother's eyes. In another, a soldier hurled a baby into the air in front of its mother and caught it on his bayonet. After Ivan showed the stories to Alyosha, he asked whether there is any possible good that he

1. Rom 8:38–39.
2. 2 Cor 4:16–18.

would accept as justification for such evil. Alyosha answered with silence. But it was not a silence that capitulated to Ivan's worldview. Rather, it was a silence grounded in his awareness that Ivan's anger meant more than his words. Set up a scene of suffering as Ivan did, and *then* import a creating and loving God into the scene and, with no other information at hand, ask the question, "Do these things fit?" The answer must be *no*. There is no other answer. Ivan went further. He said that even if God showed him how some enormous good was possible, but only if this kind of evil was allowed, he would refuse to accept it. Ivan's refusal to "accept the deal" resonates deeply with our sense of outrage at such suffering. Even the language of a "deal" is repulsive, as though the suffering of children and their mothers can ever be an acceptable currency for bartering. Within Ivan's philosophical style, refusal to accept the deal seems grounded in a sense of justice to which even God must be held accountable, if justice is to mean anything at all. It is striking that Alyosha's truest response to Ivan's dilemma was no argument at all. Rather, he went out into the world and took care of suffering children, while Ivan sank into madness.

In any case, that is *not* the universe in which Saint Paul lived. For him, there is no calculus of tit-for-tat exchanges in which various forms of suffering are traded for various benefits. He lived in relation to a loving God. This is the lens with which he *started*. Love was his fundamental reality, even as he tried to understand, or perhaps merely endure, the dark night of the soul, sorrow in the face of unutterable suffering, and, at the center of the Christian story at least, the words "My God, my God, why have you forsaken me?" There is no less suffering in such a universe. But even when we do not understand, our lament can be *lived* in relation to a loving God every bit as much as our gratefulness when beauty erupts. For someone like Paul, neither beauty nor suffering functioned as evidence in a philosophical debate. His very life was oriented toward the love of a creator to whom he was grateful for beauty and in whom he hoped when faced with suffering. Beauty and suffering were experienced from within his lived commitment, a lived philosophical style, and this way of understanding the meaning of beauty and suffering is an important alternative to a style that brackets and abstracts suffering from the fullness of a *lived* life.

Whether we are thinking about experiences of suffering, of love, or of our mind's ability to search out the realities of the natural world and other minds, the meaning of our experiences fundamentally depends on our answer to central questions about what *kind* of universe we live in. Our commitment to the answers we find is the means of testing these answers, and it *must* grow from inside our actual lived experience of beauty, suffering, and all the rest. This is why philosophical style both shapes and is shaped by our committed engagement within lived experience. Here is an example of a philosophical style that shapes experience through our commitment to it: I might live as though my mind is *not* merely a result of accidental determined natural events, but rather is a trustworthy foundation for rational thought. This commitment includes a judgment that my moral assessment of the Holocaust is not merely a statement that I do not prefer Hitler's approach to social structure. It is a commitment to living as though my sense of purpose is not an illusion. Suffering does not simply function as evidence one way or the other, for that is to revert to the language of calculation rather than relationship. To say that philosophical style is shaped by the course of my life is to say that my commitments are tested by what I discover from within lived experience of myself, others, and the world.

How do we know if we are wrong about our commitments? Experience clarifies what is at stake. It shows us the consequences of our worldview if we are right about the reality that lies beyond our own suffering, and the consequences of our worldview if we are wrong about the rest of reality. Life is lived once, and error about the reality of the universe might deepen our suffering—that is the risk. Our lives might be vastly different in one sort of universe than in another sort of universe. But we are not granted the option of living a day twice. The day passes, and when it does, the day has passed indeed. Nor are our days unlimited. Death (whenever that occurs—today, tomorrow, in sixty years) marks the end, and it approaches at the speed of one day at a time. My living of time pulls me toward that black hole relentlessly. Whether I go joyfully, fearfully, or in a raging fit, the day begins, things come my way, I act, and then the day has passed absolutely. One day closer to death. The tension in this brief interlude comes from the urgency that death creates, and many of our most important choices depend upon what kind of universe we live in. But we have no access to certainty about the central questions, so our lives are *necessarily* lived as wagers. The wager is not an option. We have no choice but to spend our days. Because we make choices from within a philosophical style embraced in uncertainty, all such spending is a bet.

Choices are not always made in response to present events. We also choose our responses to events in the past. If the universe is accidental and purposeless, how shall I respond to my own private moral failings? Should

I respond with forgetfulness? Do I have a moral obligation toward myself or only toward others? Do I ask for forgiveness, as I might do if I have a moral relationship and obligation to God? Choices may also be a response to future events. I know that I will be tempted to lie or act cowardly at some point in the future, and my future choices will be impacted by my character and capacity for virtue. These, in turn, are shaped by the choices I make now. So, whatever unknown moral struggles lie ahead of me, my choices today are in some way choices that frame and influence my future *action*. Corrie ten Boom responded to the circumstance of the Holocaust as she did because her character was shaped by her prior choices and practices of faithful response to God and to others. Shortly before dying in the Ravensbrück concentration camp, her sister Betsie said, "There is no pit so deep that God's love is not deeper still." She could say that because she understood and experienced suffering in the light of her relationship to a faithful and loving God.

This philosophical response to suffering has nothing to do with the impossible task of weighing justices and injustices in the universe to see if the net balance counts for or against the existence of God. It is a commitment to living in a certain way. It is a wager. But from inside the religious worldview, questions still hound the mind in the form of lament. How long, oh Lord, how long? Why have you forgotten your people? Why have you forsaken me? When we are shaped by commitment to this kind of philosophical style, we experience even God's *absence* in relation to the reality of God, the God whose presence we once tasted, the God for whom we now long.

For better or worse, tens of thousands of pages have been written about why there is suffering in a universe created by a loving God. But that is not our question. Our question, finally, is only this: Since we live in the local universe where beauty and suffering leave us both enchanted and in pain, how should we wager as we shape the philosophical style that frames our lives? Suffering can be portrayed on the stage, and suffering can be lived in the presence or felt absence of God. Both of these approaches address the *meaning* of suffering to us. But there is another approach to the reality of suffering that asks a refreshing question: Whatever the meaning might be, how do we focus on *solving* the unfortunate realities that lead to suffering?

Suffering as a Problem to Be Solved

Most philosophical styles are compatible with our efforts to reduce suffering. When we frame suffering as a problem to be solved, we aim to cure, not explain. Most of us would probably trade an explanation of suffering for the resolution of suffering. Even if we admire Socrates' calmness in the face of death, most of us would prefer a delayed death to a philosophical death. I am grateful if someone gives me antibiotics for my infection, chemotherapy for my cancer, or morphine for my pain. Suffering may help us learn patience, but even then we maintain equanimity *despite* the suffering. This is a very different kind of "good" than, say, love, generosity, insight, contemplation, music, or great food and wine, all of which are valued for their own sake. Suffering interrupts so many other good things. We not only welcome the relief of suffering, but we feel obliged to relieve the suffering of others where we can. We rightly have high praise for those who find new ways to cure disease or decrease suffering. Though avoidance of suffering is not the highest good on most accounts, and though there are certainly some goods for which one is willing to suffer, still, relief of suffering is a great good, all other things being equal.

There is no moral system I know of in which suffering is not viewed, at least in part, as a problem to be solved. Though suffering has no absolute scale, one fair measure is the extent to which it interrupts human flourishing, whether that flourishing is in the form of thinking clearly, playing with friends and family, or breathing freely. In such cases, the goal is to overcome the obstacles to these goods. If my eyes are fading, give me glasses. If my back hurts, so that I cannot go on walks with my dog, give me pain medication. If I am short of breath, give me oxygen. In each case I have a goal—to see, to walk, or to breathe. Those are good reasons to solve the problem of suffering. But if the goal of relieving suffering is untethered from the value of other goods, problems arise.

I am a pediatric oncologist who has spent most of my career trying to cure disease and relieve suffering. I am also a physician working in the era of American healthcare reform, a reform that has become necessary in part because the realities of illness, suffering, and death have been too isolated from other questions of value and human flourishing. Medicine is a messy, complicated endeavor full of fits and starts, but it has also led to many wonderful discoveries. Because of this, we have become optimistic that many sources of suffering can be cured through advances in medical science. This optimism grew steadily from the time of Vesalius' *De humani corporis fabrica* (1543) through Thomas Sydenham's classification of diseases and the consolidation of a scientific approach to medicine embedded in the medical curriculum developed by Herman Boerhaave. Medicine became the benefactor of humanity as it introduced new approaches to anesthesia and analgesia, as well as new promises for curing disease and lengthening life. This unabated optimism continued through the middle of the twentieth century. Questions have been raised in recent decades about how far medical science can, or should, reach. Nonetheless, the rough trajectory of optimism in medicine helps us think about philosophical style for several reasons.

One important reason is that the trajectory is long. I may want a cure for my type of cancer, but if it has not been discovered yet, my hope is not likely to be fulfilled. I will die. In medicine, "progress" generally applies to humanity as a whole rather than to individuals. Hope for progress is future-oriented, and so it only makes sense from the vantage point of a philosophical style that coherently values the future well-being of future people. This coherence assumes enormous metaphysical commitments. If I only use established technologies to cure my own disease or suffering it is not necessary for me to value other people. But research trials in medicine are designed to answer questions that are often only relevant to people besides myself, and my motivation for caring about anything beyond my own individual presence on earth is shaped by my philosophical style.

We want medicine to help us. But help us do what, exactly? The rest of the question is this: help us do what, and at what cost, and for how long? The transformation of medicine in the sixteenth century moved it past Galen's principles and put it on the path to many useful discoveries. Nonetheless, doctors were often reviled for causing more problems than they fixed, even though the proffered remedies were supposedly "scientific." But as physicians succeeded in solving a few of the problems that caused suffering, the *mask* of science became an ever more important part of their claim to authority. Lab coats and Latin phrases bolstered the impression that medical practice is fundamentally scientific, even when the impression was unjustified. The success of medical science in the development of antibiotics, vaccinations, analgesia, and cures for cancer can lend authority to other decisions that doctors make. But the question, "To what end are we solving this problem?" is not a scientific question. If we fail to see this, we make a categorical error that can create enormous new kinds of suffering.

What are the different kinds of suffering? The answer to this question clarifies the ways in which medicine can solve the problems of suffering and the ways in which it can create new forms of suffering. We suffer because of pain, and the solution is analgesia of varying sorts. We suffer because of depression, and the solution is community, counseling, and antidepressant medications. What else counts as suffering? We suffer because of infertility, and the solution may be *in vitro* fertilization. We suffer because of spinal cord injury, and the future medical solution may be to repair the damage with embryonic stem cells. Do we suffer from unwanted pregnancy? The medical solution may be abortion. Do we suffer when we want a female child and instead have a male child? The medical solution may be pre-implantation gene testing and embryo selection. Do we suffer from the destruction of our personal genetic information at our death? The medical solution may be human cloning. Do we suffer from having "misfits" mixed in with "normal" people? The medical solution may be programmatic eugenics.

The point is that there are many things that we might categorize as "suffering," and there are many ways to "solve" the specific "problems." Some solutions, such as analgesia, seem *clearly* good. But even the value of pain relief is problematic because of the important role that suffering plays in the lives of some people. I have had many patients refuse pain medicines because of their understanding of the meaning of suffering. Some solutions, such as eugenics, seem *clearly* abhorrent. But I know otherwise decent people (including a highly regarded medical professor in a world-class university) who advocate a kind of eugenics. The Eugenics Board in my own state of North Carolina was not officially dissolved until 1977. Prior to ending the program, thousands of people deemed "mentally retarded or feeble-minded" were sterilized. The problems potentially solved by embryonic stem-cell research are deep and powerful causes of suffering, but the manipulation and destruction of human embryos to solve the problems raises many questions about instrumental uses of humanity. These questions are obscured when leaders in medical science view moral reservation as nothing more than obstruction of scientific "progress" aimed at "the good" of humanity. The problem is obvious. Identification of the so-called "good of humanity" is rendered impossible when, as one prominent scientist insisted at a large conference I recently attended, people are asked to leave their "values" outside the door of the laboratory and stop obstructing progress. Really? Then what *valuable* thing are we progressing toward?

Should we leave *that* value at the door? If we do, how do we "progress" toward anything we can coherently call a "good" or a "value"? The question is not *whether* values guide our actions. The question is *which* values guide us. The question, in other words, is this: What is our philosophical style?

When we think about suffering as a problem to be solved, we discover a simple, but useful, distinction. An advance in knowledge about the facts of nature is not the same thing as an advance in knowledge about how to manipulate nature toward some end. Science discovers how nature works. Technology applies that knowledge to some end. But neither science nor technology determines which ends are right and good. When scientists begin to talk about what is best for humanity, they have stopped doing science and started doing philosophy. That is fine. It is even laudable. But there is nothing about having a talent for natural science and technology that makes the scientist's philosophical statements reliable. Scientific skill is not the same thing as wisdom about human ends. It is dangerous to lend success in scientific investigation to philosophical judgments.

One of the dangers is that assumptions go unnoticed, and therefore they go unexamined. As a result, costs and consequences can be missed, or they can be miscategorized as hindrances to solving the problem of suffering. Science as such lacks moral arguments about the manipulation of nature for human purposes, because science as such lacks moral arguments of any sort. Science and technology can discover ways to manipulate nature because that is what science and technology do. But science cannot, as science, appeal to the welfare of humanity to justify its enterprises, because arguments about the importance of human welfare are not made up of scientific propositions. Nor are arguments about human nature, decency, obedience to God, respect for others, regard for the sacred, or conservation and care for our world. All of these are philosophical or religious topics. This fairly obvious point must be made explicit, because when philosophical statements are confused with scientific propositions, the authority of the latter can bleed into the former. This can allow bad philosophy to have a lot of power in the world. Consider the development of the technologies to manipulate the Internet, clone humans, or kill large numbers of people more efficiently. Science can serve any of these goals, but it cannot tell you whether or not the goals are good. If suffering is thought of merely as a problem to be solved, without reference to questions of human nature, flourishing, and obligation, things can go terribly wrong. And when things go wrong (even as a result of the science going right) the question looms, what have we done?

This happens every day (on a smaller scale) in the hospital. Because of the history of Western medicine, suffering, illness, and death often occur within medical institutions. As medicine has increasingly adopted "scientific" approaches to problem-solving, the language of medicine has likewise become more "scientific." The details of pathophysiology are discussed much more commonly than the goals of human flourishing. Of course, because medicine is involved face to face with individuals who are suffering, there is always an element of nonscientific discourse. Some of this nonscientific discourse takes the form of ethics, focused on individual rights, autonomy, beneficence, and, to various extents, justice. Medicine tends toward specialization, so the details of this nonscientific discourse are often given to specialists called bioethicists.

Many problems remain. Two decades of working in the system have led me to think that, despite the overwhelmingly positive good intentions of medical caregivers, sequestering decisions about illness, suffering, and death within the medical institution often leads to decisions in a time of crisis that make no sense in relation to the larger picture of an individual's life, goals, and community. This is especially true at the end of life when people die secluded from their community because they are connected to a ventilator, gastric feeding tubes, and dialysis. This does not happen because of malevolence, but rather because decision-making is not guided by goals that arise from the reality of a person's own understanding of the illness experience, nor their sense of what human flourishing is. We just do what comes next. If the oxygen saturation drops, we put the patient on a ventilator. If the blood pressure drops, we start dopamine to bring it up. If the heart stops, we press on the chest, often cracking eighty-year-old ribs, making panic and pain the last experiences of an otherwise well-lived life. Hidden costs are not calculated. Certainly one hidden cost is societal as medical care consumes ever more of the nation's resources. But there are also local hidden costs such as the loss of the opportunity to do the work needed at the end of life. This work might include confession, repentance, reconciliation, expressions of love, prayer, gift-giving, remembering, vigils in familiar places, or easy visits from family and friends.

Much good comes from viewing suffering as a problem to be solved. But disconnected from the larger questions about human ends and the nature of flourishing, the efforts to solve the problem can lead to other enormous problems.

Suffering without Meaning

Whether we grapple with suffering in the language of literature, philosophy, liturgy, or medicine, we are motivated by a sense of purpose, a sense of hope that some kind of meaning will be found in suffering, or in our response to suffering. But is there ever suffering that is completely void of meaning? Is there ever suffering that lacks any connection to the memory of meaning, or even the wish for meaning? Our experience of suffering provokes plays, philosophy, prayer, sacraments, and scientific investigation of the natural world. But what happens when these ways of responding are destroyed by great suffering? If there is suffering without meaning, it is not accessible to the sentence I am writing, if only because this sentence retains a sense of order. Suffering that breaks meaning is not the suffering of one raging against meaninglessness. Rage is full of meaning. If I stand in my diminutive life and cry out against the universe, "No!" as I am subsumed by purposeless matter, my cry of "No," or of "Yes," or of "I do not care," has meaning.

Suffering that is truly without meaning dissolves all purpose or hope, and all language of purpose or hope. It lies motionless unless movement is prompted by shocks of pain, or else is pressed into deeper immobility by depression shorn even of language. It does not say yes, it does not say no. It does not resist or recoil. There is no "Please, God." There is no "Goddamn." It is isolated. It goes beyond the suffering of the girl in Ursula Le Guin's story "The Ones Who Walk Away from Omelas." In that story the bliss of Omelas and its citizens was premised, inexplicably, upon the suffering of a stunted child in a room with no light, no love, no stimulus. But even that child, afraid of the mops in the room, was still able to say, "I'll be good. I'll be good."[3] Le Guin's image comes close. But in suffering that is truly without meaning, there is no appeal to anyone or anything, there is no trade on the promise to be "good." There is only suffering. It shows up in the universe, it has no language, it has no context, and it has no appeal. Then it disappears with no day in court. There is no court.

Is there suffering of that sort? I have witnessed a great deal of suffering, a great deal of pain, a great deal of death. I have witnessed abuse,

3. Le Guin, "The Ones Who Walk Away from Omelas," in *The Wind's Twelve Quarters*.

trauma, and depression. I could tell a thousand stories. I will tell just one. My assigned patient had schizophrenia. He was in the hospital with no way out. My senior resident told me to put an intravenous line in the man. He was quadriplegic. The voices in his head tormented him. They had been with him for a long time, and they caused him so much pain that he finally decided to end his life (and theirs). He jumped from a bridge to the highway below and was hit by an ambulance. The paramedics resuscitated him and brought him to the hospital. When I met him he was lying on an air mattress without the ability to escape, or to resist, or to die. The voices continued to torment him as before. But he could, in stunted phrases, relate his story and even comment on it. I do not think I have ever encountered suffering utterly devoid of meaning. Maybe it occurred in the Nazi concentration camps. Maybe it occurred among children who were victims of devastation in Rwanda. Maybe it occurs at some point of starvation in a world of plenty. I do not know these things because I do not know how resilient our hope for relief can be. I do not know how long we are capable of muttering, "I'll be good. I promise I'll be good." This is a suffering that floats past the last lighted beacon of the language we use to express sorrow, outrage, or hope. How could such suffering without meaning ever be reported back to the onlooking remainder of humanity?

I do not know what to think about the suffering that occurs among animals. A gazelle takes off across the plain and the lion pounces. A deer dies trapped under a tree that has fallen in a wet forest. Animals are torn, thirsty, and hungry. I am horrified when I imagine a lion's teeth sinking into my belly, or a tree branch severing my aorta, and I certainly project my horror onto animals in nature. But in these cases a vaguely embarrassing idea of "natural order" feels fitting to me, even if it is not terribly consoling. At the very least it gives some evolutionary sense to the suffering. But what about suffering that leads to "productivity" instead of death? When Descartes identified animals as a kind of machine, he opened new opportunities for horror that he could not have imagined. Kant dismissed animal experience as unimportant because they are not persons. Kant's position provoked Jeremy Bentham to point out that the question is not whether animals are persons, but rather whether they can suffer. They most assuredly can.

We need not go far in exploring the use of animals for cosmetic research, crash tests, or food production to find nonlethal activities that are torture. Among humans, torture occurs only in the context of meaning—even meaning in the form of hate that is focused on a hated moral adversary. Animals have the neurological complexity that allows them to be victims of torture in a way that a plant or an amoeba cannot be. They do not, however, have the ability to generate a principled resistance, or to hope for escape and retribution. They suffer. Nothing more. When chickens have their beaks snipped off so they cannot peck themselves to death in their crowded cages where they lay eggs for a lifetime, their entire experience is suffering, from beak-clip to death. From inside the experience of an animal, where would the meaning reside when, in order to keep the meat tender, pigs and young cows are kept in cages so small that they cannot turn, or when ducks are confined and force-fed to make *foix gras*, or when sharks are finned for soup then discarded to sink in the sea? The moral quality of the action resides only in those who create or witness the suffering. It occurs inside one creature who experiences the suffering of another creature as meaningless. Meaningless suffering that follows from human desire and action impacts human meaning. Ignoring it also impacts human meaning.

How does suffering shape philosophical style? How much suffering must I respond to in order for my philosophical act to be genuine? Suffering is no longer local. Television, books, recorded lectures, public radio, and Internet websites give me an enormous amount of information about suffering, whether or not I want to see it. A few keystrokes can take me to whole lists of facts about AIDS in Africa—statistics about the numbers of adults who are infected, the number of children infected, and the predicted number of orphans who will lose both parents because of a lack of access to antiretroviral drugs. The same is true for famine, drought, and the devastating fallout from hurricanes and tsunamis. I can watch war in real time. I was in medical school when the United States began the fight with Iraq after the invasion of Kuwait. For the first time, we were able to sit in our living rooms and watch as a war took place. The bombs had cameras on them so that we could watch their approach. Some moments were especially poignant. For example, some buildings were blown up at night in order to reduce civilian casualties, because the only people likely to be inside were custodial staff.

How much suffering must I be willing to witness in order for my philosophical act to be authentic? This question is provoked by the stunning amount of information we all have about suffering in the world. Yes, it is too much. It is too much for one person to grasp, too much for one person to repair, too much for our hearts. Reported in terms of numbers, these events can only be received as we might receive factual information about the number of stars in the universe, or the size of an atom. We can see that the fact is amazing, but we cannot imaginatively grasp the magnitude. Statistics can thin out our sense of the meaning of suffering—x number of homeless, y number of orphaned, z number of starving. This is not moral failure. It is simply a matter of scale and proportion, or disproportion, as I compare reality to my own finitude. But suffering on a large scale that can only be expressed statistically might, nonetheless, compel me toward suffering as a problem to be solved. I might join the Peace Corps. I might send a larger portion of my paycheck to Food for the Poor. I might run for political office so that I can divert resources from less worthy causes to more worthy causes. I might go into medicine and heal one person at a time. I can be aware of the scale of suffering even as I create my own small, iterative, living responses to local suffering that grow out of my philosophical style.

I participate in a lot of suffering passively and peripherally. I eat eggs without verifying the living conditions of the chickens. I add to methane production and climate change by throwing away food instead of composting. I spend money on new dog chews knowing that there are homeless people near me who might benefit from the money. The list is long and it does bother me. But there are two responses to the centrifugal and dissipating forces of suffering that seem to squander the power of organizing forces. One is to ignore the suffering completely, and the other is to be undone by the suffering. We can solve some of the problems that are close at hand, but we cannot solve *all* the problems everywhere. Even so, we can be disturbed by suffering that we cannot entirely grasp or solve. Disturbance is a kind of awakening. Awakening can follow from awareness of suffering, longing in the face of beauty, the inner movement of deep love, or the urge to pray or lament. When suffering people or animals come our way, we can welcome them instead of avoiding them. We can respond to the suffering at hand, or we can work to avoid suffering. This is part of the active life, growing out of and returning to the mindful shaping of philosophical style. Mindful attention and active life combine into the fullness of philosophical style that shapes the complex reality of being in the world.

four

Being in the World

A Brief History of Being

In 1814 Adelbert von Chamisso wrote a novella called *Peter Schlemihl's Miraculous Story*. Peter Schlemihl sold his shadow for a bottomless bag of money. Unfortunately, he discovered that without his shadow he was ostracized from love and society. And so he became an observer in solitude, rather than a part of the world. He saw wonderful things and learned all sorts of facts about the world, but there was something profound that he missed, even in the middle of his life of exploration and discovery: he missed the intimacy of *being in the world* in the full human sense, the sense that illuminates beauty and suffering. At the end of the novella Peter Schlemihl tells the reader,

> I have learned more profoundly than any man before me, everything respecting the earth: its figure, heights, temperature; its atmosphere in all its changes; the appearance of its magnetic strength; its productions, especially of the vegetable world; all in every part whither my boots would carry me. I have published the facts, clearly arranged, with all possible accuracy, in different works, with my ideas and conclusions set down in various treatises. I have established the geography of interior Africa and of the North Pole, of central Asia and its eastern coasts. My *Historia Stirpium Plantarum utriusque Orbis* has appeared, being but a large fragment of my *Flora universalis Terræ*, and a companion to my *Systema Naturæ*. In that I believe I have not only increased the

number of known species more than a third (moderately speaking), but have thrown some light on the general system of nature, and the geography of plants. I am now busily engaged with my *Fauna*. I will take care before my death that my MSS. be disposed in the Berlin University. But, my friend, while you live among mankind, learn above all things first to reverence your shadow.[1]

Such is our life. We want to be fully in the world. We want to cast a shadow. If we try to isolate beauty from the rest of the experience of being in the world, we are left with a thin and false utopia. If we isolate suffering, we are consumed with a sense of dreadful vulnerability. The totality of what is real presents itself in the concreteness of individual things in a complex and mysterious world in which we also are embedded. We are engaged with, and dependent upon, a world where beauty and suffering show up together. We are not mere observers. We are fellow *beings* who cast shadows. We do not live inside brackets, and even when we bracket parts of reality for the sake of thought or action, our minds wander toward questions about the whole of reality. This forces us to acknowledge the ways that beauty and suffering are juxtaposed. Beauty is altered by the presence of suffering, and suffering is altered by the presence of beauty. This is especially true when they show up in the same place, at the same time, in the mind and life of the same person.

Questions about being in the world are not about abstractions. They are about the fullness of this tumbling and forward-moving flux I call my life. They are about what might be called *everything*. That feels vague, but vagueness is a common liability in the effort to get to this notion of being. This is one of the oldest and most important efforts the human mind has attempted: contemplation of what it means to *be*. Philosophical ideas about "being" are fascinating, but they are often obscure. The history of these ideas is part of how the concept of philosophical style first became important to humans, but I will barely touch on the history. I only want to give a feel for this centuries-old conversation. Because these ideas can tend toward the abstract and seemingly esoteric, they might distract more than they help. If so, skip to the next section.

For those who find the ideas intriguing, remember what Aristotle said when he spoke about the study of "being as such": all sciences are more necessary than this, but none is better.[2] Questions about being begin with

1. Adapted from Chamisso, *Peter Schlemihl's Miraculous Story*, 66–67.
2. Aristotle, *Metaphysics* 983a.

the obvious but surprising observation that we are in fact here. The world is as it is, though it might not have been, and might not have been as it is. Why is there something rather than nothing? This is one of the stunning core questions in philosophy, and it is a very difficult question to think, in part because it is very difficult to actually imagine nothing.

There is something rather nothing. As soon as we say this, problems and questions flood in. The "obvious" becomes anything but obvious. We are forced to use "quotation marks" and *italics* to make language express something it cannot easily say without becoming nonsense. Think about the different uses of the words *is* and *are*. We start with the universe, which seemingly *is* as a whole. It is made up of distinct constituents that also *are*. This *is* a convoluted point. It becomes more so as we drill down on things that make up the world. I can say that a gondola *is*, a painting of a gondola *is*, a relationship *is*, a state constitution *is*, a poem *is*, a musical performance *is*, an idea *is*. . . . Everything becomes stranger once I realize that the odd fact that I *am*, whatever that means, *is* the condition for my asking of such questions. Wrestling with these questions reveals philosophical style and leads to our central question (How shall I live my life?), because my philosophical style depends on what sort of universe our universe *is*.

Why is it that things *are* in such apparently different ways? We want to discover what is real. We want to do science, study history, and watch television. But if we turn to *being as such*, our questions are of a different order. When "the question of being" first dawned upon the Greeks, it came in a very reasonable form: What sort of stuff makes up what is really real about reality? Initial candidates were compelling—water, then air, and then fire. But when Parmenides of Elea noticed that all of these candidates have something in common—namely, that they *are*—he set things going for philosophy in a very new way. He saw that the fundamental stuff of reality, underlying even water, air, and fire, must be *being*. But as soon as he said that *being* is the stuff of reality, it became possible to say something strange for the first time: being *is*. This sentence is strange because it forces us to ask whether there is a difference between "to be" and "to exist." This is the kind of distinction that either enthralls a mind and leads to continued study of the history of philosophy, or else leads to the conclusion that life is short and so much can be enjoyed without ever again asking about this distinction. Aristotle agreed that these metaphysical questions are, in one sense, the most useless. But he also thought that thinking about these kinds of questions is the best act the human mind can do.

For those who still do not want to skip to the next section, there are two ways to think about the word *being* contained in that troublesome little sentence, "Being *is*." One way is to think of *that* which is. The other is to think of the fact that it *is*. For the former the mark of a truly real thing is self-identity: a thing is what it is. For Plato, the forms are the "really real" things, the things that are unified, completely and unalterably what they are. The work-a-day world of change and becoming that we actually inhabit is a shadow-world. Because of Plato's attention to being (rather than existence), he could argue for degrees of being between the forms (which are "really real") and nothing (which "is not"). Our world falls in between these two extremes. Had Plato equated being and existence, he could never have used these terms because a thing is, or it is not. There is nothing in between, so to speak. Plato was his own first great critic. In his dialogue the *Parmenides*, he proved that the idea of the self-identity of the most real (the form) is contradictory because it includes other forms. Consider the form of justice. This form shares in an idea other than itself—the form of unity. But now it is no longer unified. This point disrupted one of the centerpieces of Plato's philosophical structure. Once he discovered that his own understanding of being fell in on itself, he tried to fix things by thinking of unity, not in terms of being, but in terms of that which is beyond being—the Good. And what is the Good? Socrates, Plato's hero, refused to say what the Good *is*. He would only say what the Good is *like*. One reason for this is that the Good is "beyond being," and so it is necessarily *not* being. If this is true, then the question "What *is* the Good?" is in the wrong form. But what other form could the question have? Is the Good beyond the reach of our questioning? Is this even intelligible?

Neo-Platonists such as Plotinus answered by saying that the Good is above intelligibility, but it is still the foundation of all philosophical investigation. The Good (or the One—they are the same) is that from which all else emanates. We can only speak about the One through the *via negativa*, "the negative way." We cannot say what the One is, but only what the One is not. The starting point for this "way" is the odd claim that the One is beyond reality, beyond being. It is not properly called a thing. It is not properly called real. This is not because it lacks real-ness. It is because it has an excess of reality. Ideas like this, if they are not pure nonsense, strain language beyond its capacity to express them. I like the way Etienne Gilson stated this idea: "The One is nothing, because it is much too good to be something."[3] It cannot be thought. To say that it is beyond being is to say that it is nothing. Being comes *from* the One, so the One cannot *have* being. This is a striking shift away from "being" as philosophy's first principle. The being that all things have is not itself the One. It emanates from the One. The One transcends being. The One *is not*. This Platonic concept of being that leads to a strange absence of existence from the very source of being makes us wonder whether there is a more plausible account (and it also helps us understand why many people skip this part of philosophy). By "plausible" I mean an account of being as we experience it, or at least a concept of being that we can think, a concept of being that is intelligible.

Aristotle, Plato's pupil, thought there was a better account. In the world I never meet the form of "dog." I meet Emma and Sophia, the beagle and the English setter currently curled up on the chairs in my study. These flesh-and-fur dogs exist. Aristotle starts with them. He asks what it is that makes them real. It is not enough to talk about the coolness of their noses, the floppiness of their ears, or the length of their tails. These are features of the dogs, but we want to know what it is for Emma and Sophia to *be* dogs. Nor is their "dogness" something that exists apart from the beasts on the chairs. Emma and Sophia provide the opportunity for things to show up in my study that, apart from the dogs, would not show up—black spots, paw pads, and their doggy smell (though their smell does tend to remain after they leave the room). But what makes them real?

To be a dog is, at least, to be. A dog is a nature, capable of change, movement, and action. Dogs can act because at their core they are themselves energy, act. What does "act" mean? There is the *act* that is the act of being. There is also the *act* that is the act of eating dog food, or chewing on the arm of my chair. These latter acts are made possible by the former act. This act of being is not an idea in which Emma and Sophia participate. This act just *is* what it is to *be*. Is there anything more that can be said about what this act is? No. We cannot get behind everything. Act is given. But its givenness is right here in front of me, curled up in the chair. For Aristotle being is substance. Substance is what a thing *is*. It is not the fur and flesh that comprise the *matter* of Sophia and Emma. Rather, substance is the inner principle accounting for all the features and actions that make up the act of "being a dog," as opposed to "being a cat." This is what Aristotle calls "form." Nothing else accounts for the presence of Sophia and Emma right now other than *matter*, plus the *act* that is the *form* of a dog.

3. Gilson, *Being and Some Philosophers*, 22.

Is this true form of dog that accounts for Sophia also the true form of dog that accounts for Emma? Yes. This is what it is to be a species. Only dogs are real, not dogness. But what is most real in Sophia as a dog is what is most real in Emma as a dog. The fact that Sophia is thin and lithe while Emma is short and stubby is a difference in shape, not form. But it seems odd that what is most real about them is their species, rather than the very stuff I see in front of me—Sophia's long body and Emma's little body, the differences in their ears, the differences in their barks. Why is the form more real than the particulars of the individuals before me? What is this "form" of the species? What kind of reality does it have? Just a name? A concept? Surely it is not a reality on its own, since that takes us right back to the problems of the Platonic Idea.

Here again I find Etienne Gilson very illuminating. He thinks that the knotty problem arises because Aristotle bungled the question when he failed to distinguish between two uses of the verb "to be."[4] If "to be" means *that* a thing is, then individuals exist, and forms do not. If "to be" means *what* a thing is, then forms alone exist and individuals do not. If only Emma and Sophia exist, they are both their own species, species as distinct from each other as a dog is from an elephant. But that idea misses something important that Sophia and Emma seem to share. If the form of "dogness" exists, how can this form be united, and still exist within multiple participants, including Emma and Sophia? This is a deep problem if "essence" is the most real, fundamental feature of being. If this "form" does not subsist apart from the actual matter that makes up an individual instantiation of this being—muscle, hair, nose, and paw—what *is* it?

To move toward an answer, return to the devilishly complex phrase "being *is*." Francisco Suárez was a seventeenth-century philosopher who wrote *Metaphysical Debates*. He thought in detail about the distinction between being as a present participle (I *am*) and being as a noun. For every verb-form of being (such as the phrase "I *am*") there is a noun-form of being that signifies the thing that exists. The noun "being" refers to actually existing things, but the idea can be extended to "things" that are merely *capable* of existing. Suarez calls this notion of being "real essence." Real essence does not mean something that only shows up in the imagination. It does not refer to something that is possible merely in the sense of being noncontradictory. A real essence is an essence that is true in itself. It is capable of being actually realized. The noun-form of being includes both

4. Ibid., 49.

the *actual* and the *possible* real essences. The verb form is narrower and only refers to beings that *actually* exist. Essence is *what* a thing is. When the *possible* essence of a thing becomes the *actual* essence of a thing, and so begins to exist, its *cause* has pulled it from possibility to actuality. What is the relation of essence to existence for Suárez? Existence is what distinguishes an actual essence from a possible essence. But existence is not some additional thing added to essence. The puzzle, Gilson points out, is that "existence seems to add so much to essence, and yet is itself nothing."[5] This is the conundrum at the heart of this kind of *essentialism*. There is no distinction between "actual existence" and "an actually existing essence." Our ability to abstract "existence" from "existing essence" is nothing more than a mental exercise. The glaring problem is this: if an essence that is possible (but not actual) is itself nothing, then actualization of it is actualization of a *nothing*, and that is exactly what you end up with—nothing. The strange consequence for Suárez is that possible reality is just as actual as actual reality.[6] Essentialism reduces to nothingness the very *act* through which being actually *is*.

A radical shift occurred when Immanuel Kant took up the question of being. Instead of trying to say what existence is, Kant decided to say only what it is not: existence is not a predicate. Think of a unicorn. A unicorn has many defining features, including its single horn. Suppose we make a complete list of the predicates needed to fully describe the essence of a unicorn. The one predicate we will never find on the list is "existence." This is also true for actually existing things such as myself. There was a time when I did not exist, but my essence is in no way affected by this fact. Nor would my essence change if I ceased to exist. Likewise, the essence of a unicorn would not change if one suddenly appeared. I would recognize it by its horn, not by its existence. Whether it exists or not, what I posit when I posit a unicorn is always the same. This leaves us with the puzzle of what, if anything, existence adds to an essence such as that of a unicorn.

After saying what existence is not, Kant did not bother himself much over questions about existence. Once he decided that the world comes to us in sense and is thought through the understanding, he was satisfied to say that existence is just the fact that things that show up in sense—those are the existing things. The function of existence is very limited in Kant's philosophy. Beyond this there is not much to say—indeed, there is nothing

5. Ibid., 102.
6. Ibid., 106–7.

to say. However much reason feels compelled to ask questions about existence, philosophers are better off acknowledging their limits and turning to other topics that they can meaningfully explore. Existence does not alter the concept of an object in any way. Existence does not impact *what* an object is. Existence is only a condition for our knowledge since, without existence, there is nothing. But this condition is not itself something we can know anything about. It belongs to the realm of the unknowable. Existence is a condition for knowledge, about which we can know nothing more.

Hegel was not satisfied with this. It leaves out too much. At the core of his philosophy was the idea that the truth is the whole. Working out the nature of this "whole" involved some strange concepts cast in strange language. There is nothing in reality "as it is in itself" that is unintelligible, including Hegel's ultimate idea—the absolute. Part of his solution to the problem of essence and existence depended on the idea of concrete universals. There are concrete essences that we grasp through concrete concepts. A lot is smuggled in through this word *concrete*, though not very much is clarified by it. Of these concepts, "God" is the most concrete. God unifies all of the interrelated concrete essences as they determine, and are determined by, each other. Compared to the concreteness of these essences, the concept of "being" pales because it is so non-determined, so non-concrete, so abstract. "Being" cannot be perceived by the senses, nor can it be intellectually represented because of its utter indeterminateness and its complete lack of content. But it is nonetheless known. How? Here things get odd. It is known by being *identical* with thought. It is thought thinking itself. Being is thought as thought's own object. As such it is absolutely empty with no concrete determination. It is *no* thing, which is, of course, to say *nothing*. Being is nonbeing, and conversely nonbeing is being. The movement of one into the other is *becoming*. This motion that is called *becoming* allows these two contradictory moments—thought thinking of being as nothingness, and thought thinking of nothingness as being. In this *thought*, becoming becomes. This unity is a concrete object of thought. Essence is *thought* with *appearance*. Concrete essences are not the self-identical essences that previous philosophers described, but rather they are a unity of being and being's appearance to itself that, as a unity, becomes the thing. This just *is* knowledge of a thing-in-itself, the unity of the thing's essence and its existence. It is a complex and strange position.

Hegel's obscure unity would not stand unopposed for long. The most devoted opposition came from Søren Kierkegaard, who complained that

Hegel's great system left out the one thing that matters most—how the individual is supposed to *be*. The most important ideas are not about *knowing*, but are rather about *living a life*. Even this is too abstract. The most important thing that is absent from Hegel's system is concern about living *my* life. Kierkegaard vehemently resisted the degeneration of life into abstract speculation. Through the abstractness of Hegelian philosophical thought, the real contradictions and conflicts of existence collapse into apparent resolution. But in the course of this *apparent* resolution, the *truth* of our existence is lost. And if that is lost, what is the point of any philosophical system, however complete or beautiful it might be?

The truth may be the whole. But if Hegel's notion of "the whole" eliminates the reality of contradiction and difference among actually existing people like you and me, we will surely protest that something important is missing. If we abstract to the point that thought and things are the same, we can create a philosophy of the whole. But when I show up on the scene, only to find that I have no place in the system, I will make a fuss, because I *am* part of the whole. If there is no room for my subjective life, the system is *not* the truth of the whole. No objectification of truth can reduce my subjective reality to something that fits the system. What I assert from inside my own existence stands against the system, and it does so without apology. There I stand. My existence precedes my thought. As such it will not submit to a system of thought. If this implies a kind of loneliness, so be it. But even in that loneliness I can think about the whole. From within my existence I do not object to connecting to the whole. I just do not want to disappear in a philosophy that collapses abstractions and resolutions that depend upon the translation of existence into thought. Existence is not thought. For Kierkegaard, existence is being *engaged* in the moment as a subject, and such existence is knowable *only* from within this engagement. It is inaccessible to an objectifying, abstracting philosophy that would reify being or abstract essences. Existence stands against systematic philosophy, because that philosophical style is an obstacle to the primary goal of a human being—to exist. Only a *lived life* counts as philosophy done well. Anything else might pose as philosophy, but it is nothing more than a great thought experiment.

Does philosophy objectify reality so that there is no room for existence in its metaphysics of being? Thomas Aquinas approached this question in a way that engaged existence, without eliminating existence or resorting to the strange idea of existence devoid of being. Part of his discovery was to see a deep equivalence among existence, beauty, and goodness. Thomas agreed with Aristotle's idea that our knowledge of being is gained through a first cause ("first" in the sense of primary, not in the sense of being temporally antecedent). But faith pushed him further. The first cause through which we come to know being is God. Aristotle said that being is at least substance. Thomas agreed, but he thought there was more to the story. Aristotle thought that substances (and their essences) exist in their own right, but for Thomas substance is completely contingent. All essences are utterly dependent on their relation to God for existence. Simple substances are as substantial as Aristotle thought they were, including the fact that they endure. Simple substances do not *in themselves* have the potential to cease being. God can annihilate them, but if they are left to themselves after they are created, simple substances are eternal (unlike composite substances that are corruptible by virtue of being composites). The eternal character of such simple substances (including the souls of humans) is a fundamental characteristic of created reality. But the cause for the existence of incorruptible simple substances, or corruptible composite substances, is *outside* the actually existing substance. This is the fundamental difference between the universe of Aristotle and that of Thomas.

Why the difference? There is a crucial distinction between two of Aristotle's categories of causation—formal cause and efficient cause. Formal causes make a thing *what* it is, but efficient cause makes a thing *to be*. This is where Thomas's act of faith extended understanding beyond what Aristotle had grasped. If there is no existence, there is no substance. And where there is no substance, there is no existence. Existence is not an essence, but everything that exists has an essence. Because the efficient and formal modes of causality cannot be reduced to each other, essence and existence are distinct. These are distinct not in the sense that one being is distinct from another being, but rather in the sense that the essence defining a thing is *really different* from what makes the thing to *be*, what makes it exist. Existence is an act, *the supreme act*, of all that is. It is first in the order of reality. The *act* of a form is not itself a form, and so has no essence distinct from itself. There is no existence outside actually existing beings. Gilson states this idea beautifully: "God *knows* essences, but He *says* existences, and He does not say all that He knows."[7]

What about God? God is unique. God alone is a pure act of existence. All other beings exist because of an act they *receive*, rather than an act that they *are*. This is why they are contingent. Beings might not exist. I might

7. Ibid., 177.

not exist. But if I do exist, it is because my essence was made to *be* a being by a gift of existence. My existence is a gift. My being is both the thing I am and the act that makes me *to be* the thing that I am. This act is received from God. But for God, essence and existence are one. God is the pure act of existence. This metaphysics places me in a very different relation to the universe than the metaphysics of the One, or that of modernity, or the subdued metaphysics of a postmodern rejection of metaphysics. The metaphysics of Thomas allows us to do away with the notion of essence as some unchanging abstract entity. We can do away with the idea that essence is somehow the root of all being. The problems that follow from such a metaphysics disappear.

Thomas's philosophical style has transforming implications for my own being in the world. Yes, I am individuated by matter and determined by form (I am a human rather than a dog). But my true individuality comes from the act of existence. Why? This act—this "to be" that is me—is singular and unique by virtue of the fact that you, in your individual existence, cannot be the act that I am. This act that I am opens my eyes to the singular act that you are. This act allows me to see the way that every being is acting toward a *purpose*, which is *to be*. The world is transformed by becoming purposeful. My knowledge of the world is not a reach past the world, toward some eternal form. It is an encounter with the beings of the world in the fullness of their actual existence, neither generalized nor abstracted. It is the purposefulness of a created universe that allows the unity of being, goodness, and beauty. This philosophical style changes the way we see everything—trees, animals, stars, persons. The world is illuminated by this concept of being. Our vision of the world is redeemed. This is true of our being, and it is also true of the way we know and speak about reality. Our common-sense language is deeply bound up with the verb "to be," the copula "is." As we speak, our speaking *is* about what things *are*. The knowledge of *what* a thing is differs from the judgment *that* a thing is. We can conceive the essence of *a* being, but not that of being itself. Our *knowledge* never gets out of being. It is rooted in existence. This is what distinguishes *knowledge* from *thinking*. Thinking is knowing one's own thought. Knowing is directing the mind toward an actually existing thing, grasping its essence within its existence.

How do we reach pure existence? Philosophy can bring us to the threshold. It can show us a goal that is most worthy of pursuing. This is metaphysics. Metaphysics is fundamentally a joyful—and often strange—pursuit carried out in a world made up of beings that are, somehow, the unity of essence and existence. On this threshold we can see what it would be for a world to follow from the creating act of God, who is pure existence, a reality that is both mysterious and intelligible. Mindful awareness of existence is one way to begin defining philosophical style, even though the goal must finally be reached by means other than philosophy. The philosophical act can transform the way in which we encounter each other and the world. This deeply human act transforms the world's beauty and its suffering. Even as we come to grasp the surprising intelligibility of the world, we also slam into the universe as mysterious. Thomas thought of beauty as goodness perceptible to the senses. Only a philosophical style that views being as a unity of essence and existence, rooted in the pure act of God, could discover the identity of being with goodness, and then respond with worship. These sketchy thoughts about "being as such," and the being of particular things that exist in the world, force us toward the one aspect of the mystery of being to which we have unique access: the mystery of my own being.

The Mystery of Being Me

What are you doing?

I am writing. I am cooking dinner. I am reading a book. I am doing nothing at the moment.

When we think about philosophical style, in the lights and shadows of being among so much beauty and suffering, something important happens to us: we spend time. This obvious-sounding point, so familiar and so nearly cliché, has a surprising and even uncanny flavor that is easily lost. Whatever I do requires that I spend time. I must trade one thing for another. I trade this hour for a chance to write. I trade my day for the chance to spend time with children and families in the hospital.

This is a strange economy, because its currency is *my* time, but I have no choice about whether or not to spend it. I fill my life with whatever it is I do, and at some point I will face death. Even if I am given a reprieve, it will be temporary, because "cures" do nothing more than delay death. The currency of my time is limited and I have no idea how much of it I have. Our response to this fact shapes our philosophical style.

Whatever I may say about the states of my being, I am tumbling toward death. My days slip out from under me. Time is short and precious. And yet my boss still thinks that it is important for me to attend time-consuming meetings, and television commercials insist that my time should be traded for sitcoms (some of which I watch), fast-food experiences (which I generally avoid), and vacations (which I often have no time for).

Woody Allen once said, "I don't want to achieve immortality through my work; I want to achieve it by not dying." The desire to be immortal has a long and strange relationship with the desire to be remembered. I am forced to choose acts in the course of what I call my life, so I must pay attention to *value*. The value of my individual activities depends on the quality of the activity and the end toward which it is directed. The value of our activities, on which we spend our time, populates our history. Value is the force that shapes our story, whatever it is beyond dust that remains at the end of our time. Being in the world is a creative act. In the wake of time spent, our presence and our actions leave stories and artifacts. This affects the ways others spend their time. If I trade some of my time to enjoy my children and show them my love, this will affect the ways they spend their time now and in the future. If I trade some of my time on the activity of debasing or injuring them, this too will affect the way they spend their time now and in the future.

We exist in the middle of beauty and suffering. We leave behind a story with real consequences that become part of what others experience as beauty, and part of what they experience as suffering. I cannot stop time while I mull my own actions. I cannot cry out, "Wait, wait, I need to think about this!" To wait while I think is itself an act requiring that I trade time, taking me another step closer to my own death. Contemplating thoughts of this sort should leave me astonished at my encounters with all that *is* (myself included), with all that matters, with the meaning of everything. This is the philosophical act. This is the act of awakening to the meaning of what shows up every day as we spend our time. It is not a distraction or a "waste of time." The philosophical act transforms our vision of everything that we encounter. It is the act that keeps us mindful and deliberate as we live our lives, as we spend our time. By its very nature, it disturbs us because it forces us to pay attention to the structure of value in our lives, value set against the inevitability of death.

In some cultures, past and present, it might make little sense to press so hard on this theme of trading days for acts, the theme of spending time, the idea that I set the agenda of my day, my month, my year, my life against the reality of my death, which is approaching one day at a time. But I am writing in twenty-first-century North America where the central policy deficits in healthcare, economics, and war are, in part, symptoms of a deep failure to acknowledge and respond wisely to the reality of death.

If I were asked whether I would want to live my life over again, even if I discovered that the ontological naturalists are right, my answer would be a resounding "Yes!" In the naturalist's world my apparent "acts" occur transiently on the back of purposeless events that are themselves merely accidental. Still, given that, I would choose life. I would take it in the face of such a reality. I would value my life even in a world where we show up in the middle of nothing more than purposeless accumulated stuff. This is the best that I can do to say how deep my respect is for those living from within a naturalistic philosophical style who still try to make sense of value. But if I did discover this, it would radically impact my life because it would radically impact my philosophical style.

I love my life, but much of what I love is bound up in a philosophical style that resists the idea of a final, inevitable reduction of everything to un-conscious, non-valued matter in the void, or without the void. Void or no void—it would make no difference since nothing makes a difference once those of us who can value are gone. Even though I can say almost nothing certain about the universe, my relatively uncertain view of the universe has consequences for the thing I call my life. My life—everyone's life—grows out of philosophical style. This does not necessarily mean that toasting bread or licking stamps is affected by our view of the universe, especially for someone who does not spend much time thinking about it. Acts directed toward such local and limited ends might be the same in both a naturalistic universe and a created universe, though even small things can become loci of deep feeling and thought. If my work is to repair bicycles, the work is valuable because of the human *purpose* of bicycles—transportation, exer-cise, enjoyment. I do not need much beyond this in order for my work in bicycle repair to be understandable, enjoyable, and worthwhile to others and myself. Many activities, taken in themselves, require only a limited set of references to seem complete. House painting, weather prediction, and optometry all seem to be meaningful in light of our goals, irrespective of the kind of universe in which we live.

Other acts, however, seem aimed at ends that do depend on the nature of our universe. These acts show us why our view of the universe matters, and why the uncertain answers we offer to questions about the universe have real consequences. The profession of medicine is a good example. It is a philosophical act to say what my body is. I am a body, and this fact is relevant to everything else in my life. Because of this, the goals of medicine are always shaped within a philosophical framework. The "proper" goals of medicine are not self-evident, and they look different from the inside of different philosophical styles. For example, utilitarians frame the goals of medicine by referring to the condition and meaning of many things besides my body. A utilitarian might argue, for example, that the goal of medicine is to provide the greatest access to the most effective healthcare for the largest number of people. There are many challenges they must overcome when defining words such as *effective*, since actions are deemed effective only if they reach the desired ends, and it is very tricky for a utilitarian to say, in a noncircular way, why we should desire one end over another end. But a utilitarian would certainly not state the goals of medicine in terms of something like the "sanctity" of life.

Is the use of lethal doses of opioids and benzodiazepines at the end of life consistent with the "proper" goals of medicine? The answer to this question will be different from inside a naturalist's philosophical style versus that of a Catholic. But the stakes are high. This is true for law, politics, finance, and war. The goals are not self-evident. They depend on a larger view of the universe, a view of what matters and why it matters. If we ignore these framing questions, we risk real consequences that can lead to real harm. Of course, even the harm will be assessed and articulated in different ways depending on one's views of the universe. What constitutes harm? The answer depends upon what an embryo is, what death is, what counts as meaningful life, and so on. The answer is both a source and consequence of philosophical style. Without a certain view of the universe it makes no sense for me to become a priest, trading my days and spending my time on scripture, preaching, and the sacraments. Without a certain view of the universe it makes no sense for me to kill millions of Jews in gas chambers. "Sense" only occurs within a philosophical style. The philosopher's work is to ask, "What makes sense from within my philosophical style?" The morally courageous sequence is, first, to discern and embrace a way of seeing the universe, whether it horrifies you or fills you with joy, and second, to choose a life in light of that way of seeing.

My commitment to a philosophical style frames, forms, and emerges from my life as I choose to live it. The kind of universe I take myself to be living in also affects my own *experience* of my life. If I live in a created universe that has a meaning and purpose beyond my own personal goals, then every act, from bicycle repair to medicine, from the priesthood to child-rearing, can be accompanied by, and even transformed by, other acts, such as expressions of gratefulness to God, prayer, or lament. If my acts are gestures of obedience (or disobedience) to a creator who has some claim on me, I will choose to act or not act in light of this claim. If I live in a universe in which there is no "way things ought to be," then I will have to find a different way of making choices when I ask, "Why this rather than that?" If our very notions of purpose, value, or ends proper to human flourishing are themselves accidental and temporary phenomena that have emerged from otherwise purposeless matter, we *must* see life, love, and work in light of that conviction. We *ought* to be deeply affected by our philosophical style if we are to be honest. Of course, even the sense that we ought to value honesty requires a certain philosophical style.

You show up in the world. You must spend your time on the acts in your life. Your choices about the ways that you spend your time depend upon the kind of universe you live in. You cannot be certain what kind of universe you live in. Every moment of time you spend takes you closer to your death. You may die today. So . . . choose your life. Now. Because now is all you have.

Being as Good

Step back for a moment. If we mortals must make high-stakes choices with such little information, life sounds rather desperate. Is being in the world really like that most of the time? Even though death is unavoidable, I suspect that most of us do not usually live at this angst-provoking fork in the road between the path of "life lived in an accidental, purposeless universe" and the path of "life lived in a purposeful, created universe." Being in the world usually just means living among good things, or else living without good things, but with a sense of depravation that comes from knowing about the good things. We can experience this and never once ask what kind of universe we live in. Some things seem simply good. Some things seem simply bad.

What sorts of things seem simply good? Lists of things that seem good will vary, but friendship is a reasonable candidate. Whether the universe is created, or else is a place where consciousness accidentally emerges for a while and then disappears forever, friendship surely counts among the things that seem good about being in the world. My own list would also include things such as children, music, laughter, storytelling, exercise, sex, listening to birds, and eating good meals. Among these wonderful and simple things, *I am*, not as a question-asker but as one just *living* my life. These good things occur in my life, and I am happy about that. They populate the list I call "some reasons that being alive is good." This is regular, everyday, wonderful life.

For most people who are not living in abject poverty that interrupts even basic needs, much of what it is to be in the world involves enjoying food, friendship, and work. These are the kinds of things we call "the good things." This is the kind of list utilitarians like, and for excellent reason. However inadequate utilitarianism is as a whole account of morality, it nonetheless helps us clarify the good-making aspects of being in the world. These good things are the foundation of what I take to be the deep point of Nietzsche's doctrine of eternal recurrence, our motivation for saying *yes* to life. Even if consciousness is a scarcely registered blip on the otherwise dead eternal landscape of a meaningless universe, these good things are the reason that I would still choose to have been rather than not to have been. This choice is grounded on the concrete reality of my singular and wonderful life. Not everyone answers this way, of course. Some people commit suicide. Some people answer no, but they do not commit suicide, maybe because others would be hurt, or maybe because they hope that the future might be different from the past.

The good-making things that compel us to judge life as valuable can also distract us from important questions. Is this enough? Why am I doing this? Why am I here? Questions like these are not about the inherent value of bicycle repair, food, or friendship. Instead, they test how far this goodness goes and how much weight this goodness can bear given our strange circumstance: we show up by no choice of our own, we develop relationships with each other and with the world, and then we die, often anticipating and fearing death for decades before it comes. As a pediatric oncologist, I see this in teenagers who are dying of cancer and grappling with what to do in the meantime. Good things in a teenager's life are so often connected to the future. High school prepares one for deeper study in apprenticeships or college, falling in love anticipates the possibility of marriage, and the hope for marriage often anticipates the possibility of children. When work, marriage, and children are no longer possibilities because of impending death, it is reasonable to ask, "Why should I bother with geometry?" But there is uncertainty. I can extend the time to a teenager's death by a week, a month, a year, a decade. Does this affect the choices that count as "reasonable"?

Nothing silences the question, "Why am I here?" Not creativity, not public recognition, not the bearing and raising of children. Every good falls short, even for someone who answers *yes* to the question, "Would you do it again if this is all there is?" Anyone who answers yes to that question must find being in the world good. But there can still be a gap between the good that makes us desire to be in the world and our sense of how things *ought* to be. The gap does not come from the fact that some people do not think that being in the world is good. Even if everyone wanted to be alive no matter what kind of universe we live in, the gap would still loom between our list of the *good-making* aspects of being in the world that actually show up and our sense of how things *ought* to be. Mere longevity does not close the gap. Repetition of goods in a life does not close the gap. Death affects our philosophical style, but the absence of death would not close the gap. The absence of death would not answer the question, "Why am I here?" Why not? The reason is that it would only prolong the asking. I want to know if the good of being here is grounded in purpose of some sort. I crave a purpose connected to something that does not derive from me, my history, my body.

Those of us who are inclined to ask such questions can try to defuse the urge and just learn how to be satisfied with good things as they come. We can refuse to dwell on questions about purpose, or why we are here. But letting go of such questions is also an important way of answering them. Letting go of these questions is a way of asserting that these questions should not determine how our lives are lived. When we ask these questions, we tap into the *idea* of purpose rooted in something other than the accident of history. But in order to let go of these questions, we must already choose to believe that the universe is purposeless and accidental instead of created. If we choose instead to continue asking such questions in this mysterious and uncertain universe, it is probably true that we need some level of *commitment* to the possibility of the purposefulness of the universe as a whole, no matter what the conditions for "purposefulness" turn out to be.

If being in the world is good, it is hard to avoid asking what we mean by "being good." In my brief sketch of philosophical ideas about "being," the idea of "the Good" arose repeatedly. Socrates' idea of a "form of the Good" that exists on its own did not survive scrutiny. But Plato seemed to think that even if the idea is untrue, it is so beautiful that we must still somehow embrace it. This is illuminated by the palpable goodness that seems to subsist for many of us as a quality all its own in our universe. Our sense of purpose leads us to questions about what is truly good about being in the world. Love is the clearest window on purpose and the goodness of being in the world.

Why love? Because love is the reality that we least want to reduce to purposeless absurdity. Of all the things that are reduced in an ontological naturalist's account—stories, beauty, consciousness, reason, music—I most abhor the idea that my love for my wife, my children, my friends, strangers, or God can be reduced to accidental, unintended chemical events. Obviously the fact that I abhor it does not affect reality one way or the other. But why do I abhor it, and what do I do with the *fact* that my mind and body abhor this conclusion? The whole idea seems wrong-headed (and wrong-hearted), not merely because of some philosophical disposition to reject naturalism, but also because it simply *does not fit the experience* of someone who has loved deeply. The same can be said about other aspects of being in the world. But love resists reductionist explanations more than any other experience. Naturalism's account of love is unsatisfying, not only as an explanatory theory but also as an expression of my own radical encounter with what is most real in my life, and what is most good. Before I will relinquish something this good, an explanatory theory that reduces love (and longing, and beauty, and reason, and moral conscience, and consciousness) to purposeless chemistry is going to have to be astonishing. I cannot have chemists and physicists disagreeing with the conclusions. If I am going to accept something as profound as the assertion that chemistry or physics has eliminated nonreducible love from the universe, I am going to need robust consensus. We are nowhere close.

I would also need an equally astonishing argument for why I can trust the truth of the naturalists' rational argument since all of their arguments are produced by the same brain chemistry that produced the illusions of goodness, morality, and love. Theists insist that much of God's work is done via bodies, matter, and physical processes (such as evolution), so the physicality of the world is not the issue. But the nature of love is the fault line between reductionists and nonreductionists. Love deserves an account that fits the fullness of our experience, an account that fits *all* the "data," including our inward perspectives, our stories, and our personal experiences of love. Inward, personal experience is the only perspective from which the reality of love can be explored. The "data" are not accessible otherwise. Those of us who deny that love can be reduced to purposeless chemistry ground our position in empirical experience, while those who would reduce the experience of love to what is indifferent to love (such as neurochemical events, however complex) must do so based not on their experience of love but on their theories. Love requires the approach of a radical realist to get it right. The pure theorist must go only on faith.

Answer Nietzsche's question whether or not you would choose to live your life again, even if the universe as a whole is meaningless. What experience would motivate your yes or your no? My own worst failures have been failures of love. My greatest experience of goodness has been the goodness of love. My inclination to answer "*Yes!*" is motivated by the people I love more than anything else. Whatever lifeless, purposeless darkness might lie on either side of this ostensibly accidental appearance of my consciousness with its capacity to love, how could I not say yes to the concrete and specific wonders of the people I love? The presence of suffering or the threat of meaninglessness might send me toward a "*No!*" if there was nothing else in the balance besides transient "accomplishments" destined for the rubbish heap, or a life made up of little more than serial pleasures—having sex, eating, getting rich, getting famous. But my wife, Karen? My children, Alexandra and Micah? My parents, my sister, my friends? Given love like this, I could never say anything but "*Yes!*"

Love is not about things, experiences, or ideas. Love is about people. It is about lovers. This is the heart of wonder and conflict. When my lover is explained to me in terms of chemistry or biology alone, or when she is threatened with death, I say, "No!" My philosophical act finds its most powerful motive in love. Love is the first mover of the philosophical act because love is the end toward which the philosophical act moves. It is in love that we find the most potent bridge to being as mystery. I will be dead soon, so I do not have a lot of time to argue with bloviators. I need good arguments. So far, this is the best I can do, and it is working. Believe me if you can, do not believe me if you cannot. Oh, and good luck.

Being as Mystery

Being is a mystery. Being as mystery starts with our sense that a list of the parts of a thing leaves out something meaningful. A list of parts fails to reveal what is most real about a thing. *Reveal* is exactly the word we need. Great poetry, music, and painting illuminate the world in new ways. But something still remains concealed. There is something present but not fully known. The mystery of being will not be reduced to anything other than mystery. Since this mystery can only be touched through acts such as love, art, or contemplation, we must act in a way fitting to the subject if we want to learn more. We cannot complain that we do not see the stars if we insist on using a magnifying glass to look at them. It is simply the wrong instrument.

Love cannot reduce the beloved to biology or chemistry. Love cannot reduce a person to a function such as tax auditor or waiter or doctor. What is this irreducible remainder that love demands? That question cannot be answered in the same way that we answer questions about the biology and chemistry of a person, or the social function of a person. Being as mystery, enlivened by the reality of love, must be investigated from within experience. This is the opposite of the goal to create or discover knowledge without a knower. The strange epistemology of love explores a kind of knowledge that *is* the knower. In such knowledge—whether it is imaginative, contemplative, or prayerful—the *knowledge* and the *act* of knowing are the same, and they are inseparable from the knower as person. *Personhood* will not submit to testing by methods used to analyze a beaker full of sodium hydroxide or the sugar content of a cantaloupe.

Even if love and our sense of purposeful mystery are nothing more than one more version of how chemicals can combine in an accidental purposeless universe, our *felt need* for something more is so strange and surprising. This consciousness of wanting there to be more is at the heart of the mystery of being, and it is most evident in our love for another person. Witnesses to this mystery are ubiquitous. The desire in those who sense it is compelling. Which account of the universe has room for such irreducible mysteries while still preserving intact all the data about reality mined through the natural sciences? To answer this we must ask another question, one that only a radical realist could ask: Which theory gives the most satisfying account of the universe as a whole, including realities that are outside of us, those that are inside of us, and those that do not neatly fall inside or outside? This question is nothing other than "the quest" for philosophical style.

When someone says, "Here are all the facts," always look at the methods they used to gather facts, and ask if there could be things those methods would never be able to detect. The "world" may be all that is the case, but "the facts" are not necessarily all that is the case as long as what we mean by "facts" is nothing more than the kinds of things currently discoverable by the methods of the natural sciences. Ontological naturalism is less a conclusion than it is a starting point. It can be embraced as a conclusion only if it assumed as an axiom. But the consequences of such a conclusion are enormous, so any hidden assumptions need to be uncovered. Our vision of the world, and the meaning of the world, is utterly transformed when we move from a created universe to that of the ontological naturalist, or vice versa.

Dissatisfaction with a philosophical style is itself a clue. It may even be a saving clue. Certainty will never be the answer to dissatisfaction because certainty is not given to us in any arena beyond tautological reasoning. We always live and act based on beliefs about the world. We choose based on those beliefs. We have not been given the option to do otherwise. In this sense the theist and the nontheist, the Catholic and the ontological naturalist, are in the same boat—everyone is finally a person of faith. We decide which faith to embrace in the course of our short lives. By "faith" I do not mean a set of beliefs regarding certain propositions about the world, but rather an entire orientation toward the world. Faith is a way of being in the world, a habit of seeing. Faith in this sense is the lived instantiation of a committed philosophical style.

When dissatisfaction sends us on a search for beliefs, we aim for true beliefs, not merely comfortable beliefs. We do not want to be foolish, nor do we want to be duped. But we can be duped in more than one way, and we can be dissatisfied in more than one way. We can be dissatisfied because something is present. We can be dissatisfied because something is absent. Dissatisfaction with absence can follow malfunction (a thing does not work because the needed piece is missing) or lack of understanding (the world would make more sense if not for the absence of the thing). Some people who are faithful to ontological naturalism nonetheless sense that morality, goodness, consciousness, longing, love, meaning, and beauty all seem to hint at something more than one might expect from a universe of purposeless matter. For them, this "something more" can be experienced as a dissatisfying absence. We can resolve this dissatisfaction by saying that none of these things we seem to experience are real. The problem ends once we answer that there is no morality, no goodness, no meaning, no love. This is the sort of bold faith advocated by thinkers like Alex Rosenberg in his book, mentioned earlier, *An Atheist's Guide to Reality*. We can also say that these things are real, but that faithfulness to ontological naturalism requires simply that we answer dissatisfaction with our hope that a better explanation of *how* such real things arise in a material world will eventually be discovered. One final alternative is to embrace this dissatisfaction as a clue that the sense of mystery we experience is evidence that there might be more to the universe than the ontological naturalists can allow, even if our current science cannot detect or imagine this possibility. This is the route many theists take. But every faith, every philosophical style, forces us to make choices in the face of uncertainty.

All philosophical styles can be strengthened, weakened, or simply altered in the course of a life. Living philosophical styles must respond to scientific discoveries and to experiences that persuade rather than prove (experiences such as those of beauty, suffering, and love). Our starting points impact the nimbleness of our responsiveness to experience. Some starting points are chosen, and some are given to us through parents, culture, or tradition. The style of an ontological naturalist might be strengthened when she experiences love, and then affirms to herself that given her naturalism, this love, however enjoyable, is just another accidental event manifesting in a purposeless universe that emerged from nothing. It takes courage to affirm that in the middle of uncertainty. That courage will help her adjust her expectations and her responses to the experience so that both stay in line with the tenets of her faith in ontological naturalism. Affirming this will ensure that love does not lead to a breach in the faith through which illusions can sneak in. What kind of illusions? Well, the illusion that there is more than purposeless, accidental matter, for one. Or the illusion that my love for others is not reducible to the accidents of freedom-less physics. These are deeply engrained illusions that have confounded the entire history of humanity if the ontological naturalists are right about their facts *and* their interpretation of their facts.

A theist might likewise find similar affirmation for her faith. She loves, and then she expresses gratefulness to God for the chance to love. Her prayer of gratitude resists a breach in her faith through which the illusion that love is nothing but purposeless chemistry might sneak in. The same might be said when she is happy with the experience of a mountainous setting, or when she is frightened at twilight thoughts about death, or when she experiences wonder on a clear winter night. Her prayers of "thank you" and "help me" consolidate her philosophical style. The faith of the ontological naturalist and that of the theist will affect the ways all experiences are framed and understood. There is no escape from this through diagnostics, science, or force.

We care about the truth of things, not just the content of our longings. Longing does not warrant our beliefs. The presence of such longings makes us wonder why we have them. But if the longing for something beyond a purposeless universe is suggestive, it is also true that if purpose is an illusion, we should want to know this. If we do not want to know the truth of things, then we are not engaged in a philosophical act. We are engaged in a form of anesthesia. Young-earth creationists and ontological naturalists both take comfort in their worldviews. But both are closed to transcendent aspects of reality that do not fit their models. What if there are ways in which transcendent aspects of the world can be known? For example, the witness of the world's religions and their saints might be one way in which we come to know such transcendent realities. This witness involves the slow progress of plodding individuals in a lifetime of prayer, worship, and repentance, as well as the story-mode in which the experience of a people variably faithful to God is expressed. At these thresholds, desire for certainty is irrelevant. Such knowledge is simply not our lot. The biggest decisions about the world we live in, and how we view our place in the world, must be made on different grounds.

Others go even further. We are stuck on this tiny speck we call Earth, in an unimaginably large universe, and humanity has been on this speck for only a tiny number of years compared to the age of the universe. Perhaps we cannot legitimately generalize anything about the universe from our paltry experience. Perhaps even probability cannot be grounds for belief, since the language of probability assumes a uniformity of nature that cannot be defended with certainty in the realm of the natural sciences. How much less can be said about a transcendental realm, should there be one?

We ask questions about who we are, what our place in the universe is, and what we ought to do in light of our identity and place. These are questions that many ignore. Many of us exchange our days for what shows up next on the horizon of an unquestioned existence—the next customer, the next lover, the next television show. An ontological naturalist will have a hard time arguing against such an approach to life: once we clear the illusory gloom of imperfection, sin, and the sense of obligation to a nonexistent entity, life can be lived however we want in its transient fullness. Let us live as it *is* rather than as we might wish it to be, and let us learn to enjoy it this way. There may be unresolved puzzles about the ways matter combines to make rational minds capable of grasping physics and reflecting on the world, but there are no "mysteries of purpose." Everything is more of the same, variations on a purposeless material theme. The naturalist does not need to bother with the mystery of purpose. Without the possibility of the universe having a creator, there is no "why," there is no purpose for the whole. This can be very freeing, if it is true.

The theist likewise does not want an imposition of mere fantasies, or stories, or myths on the world. The theist wants to see the world as it *is*. He also wants to avoid acts and circumstances that diminish morality, persons, love, beauty, and the exploration of the mystery of the universe. The theist desires to fully live out a vision of reality in which, as Hans Urs von Balthasar has said, "The ever greater light into which God guides mankind is always at the same time an illumination of the object of the guidance, created nature."[8] "Illumination" is a metaphor that best expresses what the theist experiences, because it is a "lighting up" of the world—both the internal world and the external world. The source and quality of this light is itself bound up with mystery. This is a descriptive endeavor, not a normative endeavor. I am not certain which universe is real. I do know which one feels most real to me. The inner feelings of my mind and moral life resist the reduction of minds and values to accident. This *feeling* seems worthy of philosophical attention, even if the only insight it yields comes in the form of doubt about the kind of universe in which we live.

Each of us is hurled into a situation where we are confronted by questions of our own meaning. The questions show up in the middle of our mundane, daily work of living. No argument tells us with certainty whence we came or whither we go. Here is what shows up in my daily world—my mind, love, beauty, my sense of home, other persons, longing, the uncanny, anxiety, faith. These are the kinds of things that populate my own contemplation of being as mystery, a mystery that remains mystery even as it manifests as a kind of light in love, longing, and my sense of home. Feel free to add or subtract—the point is not the list. What matters is our capacity to long for the list of things that just *do* matter. This contemplative knowledge is inward, though it transforms the vision of what is out there in the world. If there is anything that qualifies as knowledge that *is* the knower, this is it.

I am embedded in the universe as it *appears*. Where else could I be? But the universe appears to me as more than the sum of data accessible through scientific investigation of the natural world. It *appears* to me as a place full of meaning, purpose, and value, independent of myself and my surrounding survival tactics. The world as it appears is the world lived

8. Balthasar, *Glory of the Lord*, 2:58.

by me, a conscious *person* responsive to form, beauty, and suffering. I am embedded in the universe of data described by science, but my conscious experience as a person is the only thing that tethers the world of data to the fullness of the world *as it appears*, the world of purpose. An utterly complete list of entities, interactions, relations, and reactions found in the natural world will never exhaust the world as it appears to me as a person, a world full of meanings, purposes, and a felt order that is repeatedly confirmed through our surprising capacity to rationally comprehend the structure of the universe. The world of appearance can be framed as nothing more than a strange fact about how we experience transient life built on the back of purposeless, accidental, carbon-based natural events. But that is a choice of philosophical style. If we choose to reject that interpretation of the inward experience of persons, a different aspect of reality becomes apparent. We see the same things within the same universe, but we see them differently. Imagine a chemist analyzing the composition of pigments on a canvas when the artist walks up and asks, "What do think about the painting?" That is a very different kind of question.

Beauty appears. Suffering appears. Thoughts appear. Freedom appears. Other people appear. I am also aware that I am one *to whom* such things appear. I appear to myself. We yearn to understand the mystery that emerges through, and dwells within, appearance. But in the end, we can still choose to reduce meaning to physics. We can say, "This is all there is, and anything beyond what is discoverable by the natural sciences is illusion." The arguments on both sides may not matter much. One who starts as an ontological naturalist will always account for "this something more" as another part of the natural world that is explorable through the methods of the sciences, not yet explained but explainable. One who starts as a theist will say that this "something more" is most fully illuminated when we propose a divine mind—or more satisfyingly for including *intent*, a divine person, God. For a theist, love makes more sense. Truth makes more sense. Value, morality, beauty, longing, joy, hope, music, mystery, and goodness make more sense. For a theist all of these make more sense in a created universe that is not accidental and purposeless. This is not a proof for theism, any more than naturalists are offering a proof when they embrace the baseline and controlling belief that finally love, value, morality, beauty, longing, joy, hope, music, mystery, and goodness are temporary parts of an accidental and purposeless universe. At this deep level it is simply not about proof. It is about lived experience. It is about experience lived as someone aware, awake, and compelled to ask questions that lead to understanding. It is about learning to see. Among persons who love, long, hope, value, create, and so forth, some insist that the natural universe is all there is. Their lived experiences lead to astonishing complexity. Others say there is more. Their experience is also a philosophical threshold from which varying accounts of astonishing complexity can be elaborated. At the fork dividing these two worlds is the person, living a life, spending time, approaching death, and doing so without certainty. Living people have no script, but many of us want to know more about this universe in which we show up. I look within, and I look out. This is what I call my life. It is my only point of departure for my search. From inside my life, I choose my philosophical style. This life is my *only* portal into reality. That is why my philosophical style matters. My experiences and conclusions can be shared in conversation and storytelling, and so they can, in a sense, become common property. But my life cannot be shared, nor can my death, nor can the value of my traded and spent days. If I want to live my singular life well, it matters what kind of universe I live in.

So much is veiled. But veils can reveal shape and purpose. Those of us who are open to the possibility of "being as mystery" will say the same for "appearances" in the world. I am even veiled to myself. But I am aware of my longing to be more than just another transient, purposeless event in the universe. Sometimes I am aware of a vague feeling for I-know-not-what. I want something beyond death. That desire feels like it fits the kind of being that I am. But I do not merely want to endure. I want to change my relationship to time and the passing of time, and also keep love, happiness, and knowledge. I want something that I can neither imagine nor say. But I want it anyway. I suppose I want to be a god. But here I am. I am a body, with all the delights and challenges of having a gastrointestinal system, a reproductive system, a circulatory system, and a nervous system. My systems are aging, they are vulnerable to disease, they are quite temporary. My body is the only platform I have for encountering wonders and declaring longings. It is a platform made of leftover boards, borrowed twine, and rusty nails. In this run-down barnyard of a life, I welcome the possibilities of redemption, renewal, and immortality. These possibilities feel fitting. Those who finally reject these ideas as wishful fantasizing might nonetheless be able to see why the ideas at least fit with our inward experience. My longing to know God is congruent with my life in a way that a longing to become a magnificent galaxy or a neutrino is not. Something about my experiences of love and meaning also fit my desire for something beyond the death of my body and the death of the universe. These desires seem fitting, even if they disappear the moment the arrangement of atoms I call "myself" falls apart and is eaten up by the soil and its inhabitants.

As I ponder this, though, I can ask someone else whether she experiences thoughts like mine. If she does, we can share a new kind of understanding about each other's experience of life as a threshold. We can share the contours of what we see light up in the world. Our experience of mystery can become more than the sum of my consciousness plus hers. Sharing of this sort can deepen the palpable awareness of mystery. This is strangely related to happiness for reasons we do not know. We can see the same objects in the world as the ontological naturalist, but our seeing is *transformed* by the risk we take in our philosophical style. The naturalist's seeing is also transformed by the risk inherent in that philosophical style. There is a radiance to the world experienced by someone who sees the world as created, a radiance pointing past the marvelous stuff through which the local universe shows up. Theists agree with naturalists that the distinction between the spiritual and the natural world explored by science is becoming less clear. But while the naturalist will conclude that the spiritual is reducible to the stuff explored by natural science, the theist will say that natural science is pointing toward the possibility of mystery as it delves ever deeper into the question, what is matter? Science is uncovering answers so strange that some physicists have concluded that the most fundamental stuff of reality is more like mind than it is like Newton's conception of matter.

What compels some people to remain open to being as mystery? What prompts them to say that there is something beyond the accidents and determined conglomerations of the natural world? What leads them to the strange thought that the universe might be created rather than accidental? When they are on the uncanny threshold of death, what makes them consider the possibility that something persists after flesh and bone and sinew have fallen away and turned into soil? I think the answer is rooted not only in a sense of longing, a moral sense, or a capacity for rational thought and imaginative exploration, though each of these might be a clue to reality if the universe is more than a naturalist claims. The answer is rooted in the sense that we are at the very start of an adventure and that we have hardly begun to grasp the scope of what lies ahead. If the universe turns out to be more than the naturalist accepts, the most exciting questions are not about how longing, morality, and reason arise on the back of physics, chemistry, and biology. The most exciting questions are quite different. What kind of reality do these experiences point toward? What do these experiences mean? What purpose do they uncover in the universe?

Only a *person*, only someone capable of *intending*, can *mean* something in expression or creation. This is the reason that the central act that opens us to mystery in our universe is love. When someone loves someone else, a *person* is responding to a *person*. The presence of a beloved person resists reduction to purposeless molecular events determined by prior, accidental events much more than our capacity to reason or make moral choices. To love while believing that the beloved can be reduced to chemistry without remainder is to *choose* ontological naturalism as a philosophical style, and to *choose* it in the face of experiences that seem to me to beg for more. This is a deep act of faith, one that easily rivals the faith of the saints who believe in God despite apparently random suffering.

Any naturalist who acknowledges the pull of "something more" when they love has access to the kernel of what motivates all openness to the possibility of other mysteries, including the possibility that love is at the very heart of the universe, love in the person of God. This also requires faith, of course. Theists claim that this act of faith is itself a means of becoming more *aware* of the person toward whom the act of faith is directed. Theists claim that this faith is the way that spiritual reality and God's illuminating presence are revealed. Faith is not merely a set of beliefs but an act of orienting ourselves toward the possibility of God and the meaning of that possibility for a well-lived life. This is one characteristic that distinguishes the *faith* of the theist, categorically and qualitatively, from the *faith* of a naturalist. The faith of the theist is an act involving the capacity to love in response to whatever claims a creator might have on creatures like us. The act of faith is inseparable from the act of love. I grow in my understanding of this act of love by learning to love other people. For this reason love is central to a philosophical style that sees the universe as both comprehensible and mysterious. Many people convert from one view to the other, in both directions. Questions regarding the reasons for such conversions are themselves interesting and complex. Whether one is converting, or just embracing one's current view more resolutely, the notion of this move as a gamble is useful, if only because of the uncertainty and the stakes accompanying either move. Grasping the truth of our situation in this life demands that we see the importance and necessity of a genuine wager.

five

Wager

Pascal's Provocation

A while back, we left a ten-minute consciousness hanging in its final minute of existence. At first it was only aware of beauty. But in the last minute, it became aware of its own impending demise. It felt the onslaught of wonder, longing, and dread. What questions would occur to this lonely consciousness on the threshold of its death? The consciousness knows its time is short, but it will surely want that last minute to be as great as possible. How will it decide the best way to spend its last minute? If there were two consciousnesses, what would they talk about as death approaches? Those are the kinds of questions that fuel the wager.

Blaise Pascal introduced the wager as a pragmatic argument for the rationality of living as though God exists. For many, the wager seems at first like a crass, selfish, utilitarian bet aimed at gaining beatitude. If you wager that there is a God, and you are right, you go to heaven, but if you are wrong you merely disappear. If you wager that there is not a God and you are right you disappear, but if you are wrong, you go to hell. Weigh the risks and benefits and you will see that it is more rational to wager in the direction of God's existence. But this reading of the wager creates more of a paradox than a solution: if heaven is the kind of place where selflessness, humility, concern for others, and love for God are valued, it is hard to see how a scheme aimed primarily at gaining infinite benefit for myself improves my eternal prospects. However, read in the context of the whole of the *Pensées*, the wager has a very different character.[1] The benefit that makes the choice rational is the possibility that this wager is a *condition* for finding truth. Pascal frequently discusses the struggles that beset humans, caught as we are between beauty and suffering as we face life choices with so much uncertainty and so little time. Pascal's notes, the *Pensées*, are a starting point for responding to the questions and uncertainties about beauty, suffering, and being in the world. They keep our focus on shaping our lives through our philosophical style. When we wake up in the universe, we ask three questions that are useful for mining the *Pensées*:

1. Who am I?

2. Where am I?

3. What should I do now?

Discussions about philosophical style can become abstract. These three questions pull us back to the concrete particulars of our lives—your life and my life. Pascal's wager makes us pay attention to these questions instead of ignoring them. He wants us to engage with our own lives. The wager leads us to a new starting point, not to an answer. Think about these ten fragments from the *Pensées* that set the stage for the wager:

1. The power of flies: they win battles, prevent our soul from activity, devour our body. (56)

2. *Thinking reed.* It is not in space that I must look for my dignity, but in the organization of my thoughts. I shall have no advantage in owning estates. Through space the universe grasps and engulfs me like a pinpoint; through thought I can grasp it. (145)

3. There is enough light for those who desire to see, and enough darkness for those of a contrary disposition. (182)

4. It matters to the whole of life to know whether the soul is mortal or immortal. (196)

5. A human being is only a reed, the weakest in nature, but he is a thinking reed. To crush him, the whole universe does not have to arm itself. A mist, a drop of water, is enough to kill him. But if the universe were to crush the reed, the man would be nobler than his killer, since he

---

1. Pascal, *Pensées*; paragraph numbers will be cited in text.

knows that he is dying, and that the universe has the advantage over him. The universe knows nothing about this. (231)

6. The eternal silence of these infinite spaces terrifies me. (233)

7. All their principles are true, the Pyrrhonists', the Stoics', the atheists', etc. But their conclusions are wrong, because the contrary principles are also true. (512)

8. Incomprehensible that God should exist, and incomprehensible that he should not; that the world should be created, that it should not; etc.; that original sin should exist, and that it should not. (656)

9. The heart has its reasons which reason itself does not know: we know that through countless things. (680)

10. Imagine a number of men in chains, all condemned to death, some of whom every day are slaughtered in full view of the others. Those who remain see their own condition in that of their fellows, and looking at each other in pain and without hope, await their turn! (686)

Who Am I?

When Socrates stood on the steps of the temple at Delphi, the oracle said that he was the wisest man of all. He was the wisest man because he knew that he did not know. He was aware of his own ignorance, but he longed for real knowledge. The words "know thyself" were inscribed on the temple. This injunction became the foundation for the most fundamental question in philosophy. Who am I? Awareness of our own ignorance is the starting point for all true philosophy. In the course of his philosophical quest, Socrates was careful not to mistake some part of the truth for the whole of truth. Over and over he saw his fellow Athenians trying to appear wise based upon their partial grasp of truth. Socrates would have none of that. Wielding the philosopher's primary tool, the question, Socrates tested every claim to wisdom, whether the topic was justice, beauty, knowledge, or love. His interlocutors' reputations often did not fare well. Socrates was genuinely interested in knowing the truth and pursuing wisdom. But he was also devoted to his fellow citizens whom he loved. Their pursuit of wisdom was hindered by their premature and mistaken *claims* to wisdom. He wanted to awaken them and set them on a path to true knowledge. This awakening was not always well received. The same stumbling blocks arise in religious accounts that make unwarranted claims to exclusive knowledge of God, and in naturalistic accounts that make sweeping claims about reality without recognizing how far beyond science such claims go. Pascal wants us to look at the consequences of our philosophical style as we ask a central question: Which account of reality fits our lives most fully, most satisfyingly, most convincingly, and most rationally (12)?

When we try to answer the question, "Who am I?" we quickly encounter obstacles—obstacles that are sometimes hidden from us. We are distracted not only by harmful things but also by our inordinate attention to things that are themselves good. Competition in the workplace, video games, and complex retirement plans can make distraction seem like a uniquely contemporary problem. But the same was true of Pascal's contemporaries: "Take away their distractions and you see them wither from boredom" (70). He wrote that sentence in the mid-1600s. Hollowness is uncovered in the absence of distraction. We witness our own unbearable sadness when we lose our distractions and are forced to contemplate ourselves. This motivated Pascal's tumbling exploration of the world and our place in it.

Our smallness and our gossamer ties to life itself provide the backdrop for his open-ended responses to the questions of life in the middle of inevitable uncertainty. We can *think*, and this is the heart of our strength. But we have five frailties—physical weakness, boredom, distraction, slowness to learn, and fear. We are physically frail and susceptible to death. Like any other beast, we can be torn, starved, and dehydrated. We are wholly animals by nature, but we are strange animals (523). We realize that we are kin to the raccoon dead on the street, the deer running in the winter forest, and the fish swimming in the stream, but our very limitations bring to our minds the concept of *finitude*. Finitude leads us to the concept of *finitude plus one*. From there we find our way to the concept of *infinity*. Our capacity to think about such a concept reveals something important about us. From within the ontological naturalist's philosophical style, the response to this strange reality must be, "Yes, it is *amazing* that meat can contemplate infinity." Full stop. It is not difficult to see the appeal of this belief. Even for those who dare to believe in a soul as a placeholder for the *we-know-not-what* that makes us more than mere animals, weariness eventually comes, forcing us to let go of high thoughts, and we fall back to sleep where we spend half our lives. No longer able to grapple with truth or goodness, we lie there dreaming, vulnerable to the predator, drifting away with regret that our resolve seems so often to fail. Because of this, someone who believes in the soul can still see reasons to doubt. We have no control over our eyes closing. We do not merely go to sleep. We do not merely drift to sleep. We *fall* to sleep like a rock dropped from a bridge (164).

The weakness of our animal flesh is accompanied by the frailness of our grasp on the intelligible. As individuals we have scarcely a morsel of being. Even the little bit we have hides the truth of the universe as much as it reveals it. We discover that the Euclidian geometry governing our tiny experience of the world is not the geometry of the universe. We want to know more, but if a professor talks too long about philosophy, physics, biology, astronomy, or human behavior, we forget the beginning of the lecture by the time we reach the end. Midway through the lecture our stomachs growl and embarrassment makes us miss the most important points. We are easily confused and easily lulled to sleep. We want to grasp truth, but Pascal says that "our intelligence holds the same rank in the order of intelligible things as does our body in the whole vastness of nature" (230). Moreover, we are going to die soon, but we know less about death than anything else in our past, present, or foreseeable experience. We do not know where we came from and we do not know where we are going.

All of this is true. But the weird thing is that I can actually *think* about these issues. It is hard not to think about them, even if I do not want to. We think, and think, and think. Thinking motivates church, philosophy, medication, and suicide (681). Sometimes we need relief from these thoughts. We crave distraction from mortality: "It is easier to put up with death without thinking about it, than with the idea of death when there is no danger of it" (170). When I am not distracted, I trip over the idea that I am going to die, and then I tumble on to the disorienting idea that one unfortunate black widow spider bite on my father's arm, or a single misstep in the subway by my pregnant mother involving a bus or train, and I might never have existed (167).

I might never have existed. But look! Here I am!

Sure. We breathe, delight in the clouds, enjoy good food and wine, and laugh with friends and family. Yay for us. What is Pascal's response to the wonderful fact that we have shown up against all odds? "It is beyond doubt that this life's duration is but an instant, that the state of death is eternal, whatever its nature may be, and that therefore all our actions and our thoughts must follow such different paths according to the state of that eternity that it would be impossible to take a sensible well-thought-out step without measuring it against the aim of the point which must be our final objective" (682). Whatever joy we have in being alive, this life is hardly more than never-having-been if we think in terms of duration. But death is forever. If life is to be lived reasonably, then, it must be lived against the infinite stretch we call death.

This is the point in the argument where many reasonable people conclude that Pascal himself could have benefited from more distraction. His diagnosis of the human condition is so bleak and dismal. He is also somewhat dramatic as he provokes and prods us to ask about who we are, where we are, and what we ought to do. Why does he do this? Pascal thinks the stakes are so high that asking these questions is the most important work we can do. He thinks that any life not lived in this way is pathetic, irrational, foolish, and wasted. But the end toward which his argument moves is not so dark as it may seem. Yes, he thinks that the fire of his rhetoric and the shriek of his philosophical siren are needed to overcome the inertia, noise, and distraction that keep us from the most important things. When an ironic world-weary gaze deflects Pascal's shrill rejoinders, he considers this nothing more than another obstacle to be overcome. Irony is one more way to avoid what matters most. He is so set on waking us from our slumber that he will even use our need for distraction to lure us away from distraction. Human beings cannot stand tranquility, so Pascal riles us just to get our attention. We cannot stand to be bored. So Pascal gives us something to gawk at. He distracts us with spectacle. He fascinates us with extreme statements. Pascal is a tragedian and a trickster. He fills his strange philosophical tragedy with characters that grab our attention so that we cannot help craning our necks to look, only to be shocked when we see that the fascinating horror we are staring at is actually a mirror, and we are looking at our own reflection. Emptiness, nothingness, boredom, gloom, and despair all wait in the wings for their turn to appear on Pascal's stage. His is a play where an intermission would be most welcome. But it does not come. And he presses on.

We cannot even sit quietly in a room. We sail to foreign lands even though we know they are like our own home port. Why do we sail anyway? Because they are *elsewhere*. We must sail *elsewhere*. We must go to war. We must conquer nations. But once we arrive at the new port, the newly conquered nation, or the new planet, we are still unsatisfied. We do not settle in the harbor and enjoy what we have conquered or discovered. Soon after we arrive, we plunge into the next conquest. We plunge as though the conquest is *worth* plunging toward. But if the conquered harbor is only a stepping-off point for conquering the next harbor, why are we fooled into thinking that *any* future harbor is really different from the one we are currently standing on? We are bored. We need a cure for boredom. In the middle of struggling with desire, beauty, purpose, suffering, and death, we find a solution: "The slightest thing like tapping a billiard ball with a cue is enough to distract them" (168). Distraction to distraction, misery to misery, we tumble toward an eternal death. But we pursue happiness anyway, looking for something that might be our true good, looking for *anything* that might answer the open and consuming vacuum in our lives. Our longing seems *meant* for some true satisfaction, but it finds only one unsatisfying distraction after another. Pascal's curious list of distractions includes "stars, sky, earth, elements, plants, cabbages, leeks, animals, insects, calves, snakes, fever, plague, war, famine, vice, adultery, incest" (181). For him the urgent drive to find our true good does not reside in some noble quest. Instead, it devolves though a downward cascade of pleasure toward our own destruction and dissolution. This vulnerability extends even to those who do not fall down the tiers of human dissipation, and who instead—with equally colossal dissatisfaction—pursue a life in search of "truth." The mightiest intellect holding sway over universities, cities, or nations can be disturbed by a fly buzzing in the lecture hall or the boardroom (81). We may think we are proceeding according to reason, but we can be turned from our purportedly reasoned inquiries by imagination, bribes, or the theatrics and masks of authorities—the doctor's white coat, the professor's cap and gown, the judge's long robe. Pascal asks, "Who can be unaware that the sight of cats, or rats, or the crunching of a piece of coal can unhinge reason completely?" (78). We may be thinking reeds, but because we can be diverted from reason by the sound of a broom on a carpet, or by a picture hanging slightly crooked, we must hear both parts of his epithet describing our true nature—we are *thinking . . . reeds*.

Who am I? The question leads us to biology, meteorology, astronomy, and all the other sciences. At the very least, we are bodies who flinch at the thunder and gasp at the stars. The question also compels us toward metaphysics, toward asking what might lie beyond the world we see with our eyes and our scientific instruments. We ask whether anything lies beyond the world that we see with our eyes because we are aware of our own hidden inner world of love, beauty, shame, wonder, and longing that can never be reached by any measuring instrument. We ask this speculative metaphysical question, even if our speculative metaphysical answer is finally, "Nothing lies beyond." The philosophical act we call metaphysics can lead to proofs so convoluted that even when we grasp the proof, we still wonder if somewhere, in one of the many steps, a mistake was made, so that the argument proves nothing true at all (222). It does not matter whether we are Gaunilo using the "lost island" to argue against Anselm's ontological argument for the existence of God, or Bertrand Russell throwing his pipe tobacco in the air when, for a two-hour stretch, he thought that Anselm's argument actually succeeded in demonstrating the existence of God. But if intricate and well-reasoned arguments will not give us secure conclusions about fundamental questions, how can we ever find philosophical grounds that are stable enough for us to rationally choose a way to live? How do we ever commit to a philosophical style?

Demonstration is not what persuades us. Few people have the time, attention, or patience, much less the skill, to follow lengthy philosophical arguments. Even where a demonstration is provided, it persuades only the mind. Instead, Pascal says, we are usually moved by *custom*, whether we are talking about religion, our fate after death, or the probability of the sun rising tomorrow. Proof and demonstration might contribute to the force of our habits and customs, but the proofs themselves do not get us to practical conclusions that guide our lives, and most of the "proofs" are inconclusive anyway. Custom makes us more firmly theists, custom makes us more firmly atheists. "We are as much automaton as mind" (661). Neither do we really want to know the truth, especially the truth about ourselves. We would rather be flattered and deceived than to bear the full answer to the question, who am I? Those who disabuse us of our persistent illusions are loathed because they threaten our more harmful forms of self-love. "Mankind is therefore nothing but disguise, lies, and hypocrisy, both as individuals and with regard to others. They therefore do not want to be told the truth. They avoid telling it to others. And all these tendencies, so remote from justice and reason, are naturally rooted in their heart" (743).

Pascal looked at the truth of himself and he became frightened. The contingency of existence is unnerving. We are terrified by the silence of the universe in which we are tucked off into some minuscule corner, lost and without any clear reason for being here. We have no clear idea of what, if anything, we are supposed to do, "like someone taken in his sleep to a terrifying, deserted island who wakes up with no knowledge of what has happened nor means of escape" (229). In the middle of this dread, Pascal is shocked by the ways that humans respond. Instead of despairing at their disorienting wretchedness, they seem to have found a few pleasant baubles and pastimes, and having become fond of these playthings, they seem disinclined to bother with the fundamental questions of who we are, where we are, and what we ought to do. He is bewildered by this apathy. Surely we should care about whether or not there is more to life, whatever the answer may be.

When Pascal sees that we satisfy ourselves with glitter and paste, he tends to become hyperbolic. "There are only three kinds of people. Those who serve God having found him; others who spend their time seeking him who have not found him; and the rest who live without seeking him nor having found him. The first are reasonable and happy, the last are lunatic and unhappy, those in the middle are unhappy and reasonable" (192). Those of us who live in between the types wince at these unfortunate substitutes of pith for complexity. The fact that Pascal so clearly understood the human condition makes it worse. But despite the bluntness of this generalization, Pascal lunges at us because he thinks we *can* be confident about which "uncertain option" is more rational to embrace (496). In our search for happiness we seek satisfaction in wealth, sex, security, and fame. But those are no more satisfying than an inward mythical font of goodness (176). Nonetheless, only a fool or a lunatic would stop searching, simply because there might be more to the world than stuff that comes from nothing through purposeless accident. God is *possible*, and that possibility places immeasurable weight on the balance we use to judge the probability of which choice is more rational.

We oscillate between our pursuit of external satisfaction and our desire for internal equanimity. This oscillation is part of the process of discovery. It reveals our ignorance, an ignorance that is neither inexperience nor stupidity, but rather the wise ignorance of self-awareness in which we finally know that we know nothing (117). Our greatest danger is that we will "succeed" in a false world, moving from one ignorance to the next, deluded into thinking that we *do* know the world, that the pittance we call "our knowledge of the world" is the whole truth. We have partial truth at most. But even partial truths can only be *fully* understood in relation to the whole truth. Since we do not know the whole truth, partial truths can become worse than falsehoods by leading us into unwarranted claims to complete knowledge, especially if the partial truths allow us to do really cool things such as keeping massive metal tubes in the air while serving wine and salmon aboard. The appearance of knowledge leads to a vanity that is both pathetic and ineluctably knit into the fiber of our hearts (520). We write, converse, and teach about the strange wretchedness of the human condition. But in the midst of the uncertainty of our lives and the urgency of our choices in the face of that uncanny terror we call death, we attend cocktail parties and book signings organized to ensure that people are aware of the profound points we make in our books and speeches about the emptiness of human pride and the vanity of human claims to deep knowledge of the universe (521). Even in the middle of terror there is some measure of hilarity. We need relief sometimes and the comedy of our ambition fits that need.

Do we, or do we not, have purpose? Strange things happen when we ask this question. Even if we think that our sense of meaningfulness is an illusion or a byproduct of evolution, the language of purpose is tenacious. We are compelled to eat, have sex, build shelter, and kill our enemies. Is the purpose of this to continue the gene pool? Perhaps. We share this compulsion with nearly every creature, including the weeds that choke our gardens to survive. Is there anything that is essential to being human? Well, whatever intelligent and purposeful activity we find in other creatures such as elephants, whales, dolphins, and chimps, it is not absurd to suggest that humans seem *made for thinking* (513). "Thinking" in the relevant sense includes our rational engagement with the order of the world, our imaginative exploration of philosophical possibilities, and our ability to relate in love and friendship to other thinking persons. When we mourn for people whose brains are injured, we are grieving their loss of the ability to think in this rich sense. Of all our abilities, thinking is surely one that we are reluctant to reduce to accidental, purposeless stuff. How can mere matter come to understand itself? Our reluctance is not based on certainty, because maybe thinking *will* turn out to be reducible in this way. But for now, considerable faith is required to believe that accidental, purposeless matter comes to understand itself on its own (230). This belief can only be assumed, not demonstrated.

Still, we do have this amazing ability. What do we accomplish with it? Well, much of the time we use our astonishing gift to make money, gain power, win fame, and get laid. Our dignity may consist in thinking, but when this strange and wonderful capacity for contemplation, self-awareness, exploration, and rational thought is used to accumulate shiny pieces of metal, pimp prostitutes, or invent more efficient ways to kill large numbers of human beings while leaving infrastructure undamaged, our strange and wonderful ability becomes lowly, ridiculous, and contemptible (626). Or rather *we* become lowly, ridiculous, and contemptible. If this is true, then we need to know how a worthwhile use of thinking is distinguished from a debased use. If we want to say that there are better and worse uses of thinking, we need an account of human purpose and flourishing. Without this, we have no *reason* to say that the use of thought to cure childhood cancer is any better or worse than the use of thought to design sadistic pornographic websites.

Thought is a part of our dignity, but we do not explore the world only through thought. Our starting point is often a *feeling*, even when we are thinking about ideas such as space, time, and infinity. Pascal was a mathematician who understood the ways that minds intuit mathematical truths and other thinkable realities, only later working out proofs to make those insights, feelings, and intuitions explicit. This humbles our tendency to exalt discursive reason, compared to other ways of knowing through feeling and imagination. Pascal wished that we never had to reason about things. He wished that we could just feel and intuit the whole truth (142). But we must think as we can, plodding along step by step, grabbing whatever crumbs of truth we can scavenge in this short life. We know so little. In the darkness, we are happy for any inkling, any morsel of knowledge. If we are also given the chance to love in some small way, we rejoice. But we must stay humble about our modest gains (182). We can know a little and we can love a little. However, we will never have certainty about the whole truth. Our quest for the truth nonetheless brings us a kind of tranquility. If we fail to embark on the quest, our lives will turn hollow and unsatisfying.

What should we do with our lives? This is the question that burns in our hearts. Pascal's argument is moving toward an answer to that question, even if it only moves by fits and starts. In the end, the argument depends on the answer to an odd question that ultimately motivates the wager: Is it probable that probability brings certainty (496)? This seems like an absurd little question given the stakes—life versus suicide, fidelity versus promiscuity, almsgiving versus Wall Street greed. His answer to this question is yes, but he gives the answer a quirky form: as you choose the philosophical style that will shape your life, there is something at the heart of this act about which you can *probably* be *certain*. Strange. To understand his point, we first need to hear his thoughts about the second question: Where am I?

Where Am I?

Pascal is acquainted with terror. He wakes up. He looks around. When he asks who he is, the answers he discovers are not very comforting. First, he is a being who *will* die. Second, he is a being who *knows* he will die. He lives, briefly, in a world embedded so deep in the massive universe that his sense of being lost is sharpened with every glance through the telescope. Inside this world, his island home, flies can kill us with a bite and devour our bodies when we are dead (56). The biological processes involved in this devouring are the subject of grant-funded studies. The evolution of the fly is taught in freshman science classes. We can grasp the ecological balance between ourselves and biting flies. But after we have catalogued all the facts about human bodies, fly bodies, and the environment in which they meet, and after we have uncovered the mechanisms by which the fly kills, and after we have devised our best theories about how these mechanisms evolved over millions of years in disparate parts of nature, we still do not know the purpose of nature, nor even whether it has a purpose. We do not know where we came from. We do not know where we are going. Nature does not, and cannot, answer the question we most want answered: *Why?* (281). Our interrogation of nature *never* yields purpose. It can only yield mechanism. This is why ontological naturalists are full of wonder. Our ability to ask "Why?" is the single strangest thing to emerge from a universe that is utterly and eternally incapable of answering the question. And yet the question is irrevocably present.

So Pascal urges us to let go of local distractions and to ask where we are. When we brace ourselves and open our eyes, what do we find? First, the words *big* and *vast* are woefully inadequate for describing the universe. We must think of the earth as mere pinpoint, a dot beside the massive sun around which we travel. We must then imagine the sun as a mere pinpoint among countless such stars burning in the universe. We must stretch our imaginations until they reel at the dimensions of the universe, and then we must understand that we are still far from grasping our diminutive size compared to the expanse of the universe. "The whole of the visible world is merely an imperceptible speck in nature's ample bosom, no idea comes near to it. . . . It is an infinite sphere whose center is everywhere and its circumference nowhere" (230). This mid-1600s perspective on the universe has certainly been enriched and clarified by the science of contemporary astronomy, but it is a perspective that is not fundamentally different from our current concept of the universe. Pascal's perspective underscores the strangeness of the idea that contemporary scientific exploration of the universe with its billions and billions of stars somehow introduces a new piece of information informing us about our relative position in the universe, silencing provincial arguments that follow from ignorance of science. No, this view of the universe has been around for centuries, though we continue to add to the picture through discovery.

Such is the expanse of space. What if we go the other direction and consider our bodies? We find yet another infinity, yet another abyss. As we move down to hand, to fingers, to tissues, to organelles, to molecules, and to atoms, Pascal wants us to lose ourselves in astonishment at their unimaginably minute size. Holding our minds before an atom, "let us see in it an infinity of universes, of which each has its own firmament, planets and earth in the same proportion as in the visible world, in this land of animals, and ultimately of mites, in which we will find the same as in the first universe, and will find again in others the same thing, endlessly and perpetually" (230). When we interrogate the limits of division within our own bodies, the height of our conscious experience over the vast universe that is our body is dizzying. Our bodies comprise an incomprehensible number of parts, descending all the way down to quantum entities that function in a world with little obvious connection to the world as we experience it, despite the fact that in some way these entities make up our bodies. The consciousness that I call "I" is caught between two infinities, one unthinkably large, and the other unthinkably small. We are practically nothing compared to the size of the universe, and we are massive compared to a single atom in our bodies. Our bodies are strange because they are "ours" in some sense, and yet they are made up of so many mysteries far beyond our knowledge or control. Even the fact that they are carbon-based is fascinating since carbon is forged only in stars. Our bodies are made of stardust. This is why Pascal is skeptical of any totalizing claim to knowledge about *what* we can know and *how* we can know. Ontological naturalists must acknowledge the extent of their assumptions when they make claims that not only go beyond the evidence we actually have, but that go well beyond all the evidence we can *ever* have using their own criteria for "legitimate knowledge." At least theists can identify a potential piece of data that could ultimately confirm their claims: they might die and see God.

These ideas about our place in the universe are important for several reasons. The first is that they deflate pretensions common among people who tend to show up in fundamentalist groups. Fundamentalists are people whose epistemological *confidence* reaches beyond the reserves of their actual knowledge, whether they are religious fundamentalists making unwarranted but sweeping claims about the universe on television and in books, or naturalistic fundamentalists making equally unwarranted but sweeping claims about the universe on television and in books. The second reason these ideas are important is that they establish the background against which unavoidable choices must be made in my life and in yours. They *must* be made, because even refusing to make a choice is to make a choice. The third reason these ideas are important is that they were written nearly four centuries ago, and this undercuts the stupendous arrogance that leads us to think that our scientific advances place us in a position to judge religious activity as pointless and the possibility of God as irrevocably foolish. The only starting point Pascal needs for his argument about choosing philosophical style is the fact that we live between dual infinities, with uncertainty and fallibility as our lot. Our choice of philosophical style is finally bound up with the philosophical question Camus considered most fundamental: Why not commit suicide?

We live our lives between infinities. These infinities can be partially characterized by natural science, but science can never unveil origin or purpose. Between these two infinities, consciousness *seems* different from the other stuff we find in the universe, and *our own* consciousness seems distinct from the apparent consciousnesses of others. Many ontological naturalists agree with this point, and their challenge is to explain this *apparent* difference between minds and everything else. If reality is no more than an accidental, purposeless eruption from nothing, the existence of minds capable of comprehending the ideas of infinity, morality, meaning, and beauty *seems* somewhat surprising. But however great the difference appears to be between minds and everything else, Pascal thinks this difference is dwarfed by the distance between the act of thinking and the act of loving (339). Even if the gap between the mind and the natural world were narrowed or obliterated, the strangest and most surprising thing about the universe is not the presence of minds, but the presence of love. Love provides a litmus test of sorts because it is experienced by many as something that uniquely opens up the world of meaning from the inside. Love was at the heart of Plato's experience of spying out wisdom. Love was at the heart of Thomas Aquinas' understanding of how we come to see God most fully. Love is the reality we are most reluctant to reduce to accidental, purposeless events.

As we try to answer the question, "Where am I?" the natural sciences tell us most about astronomical and quantum infinities. But as thinking beings, and as beings capable of love, we know there is another reality in the world. We know the world is full of value that makes things more or less matter. Many accounts of value turn on the idea of happiness and the good life (18). As we pursue knowledge, wealth, sex, and power, this universally valued thing, happiness, remains elusive. We are left unsatisfied. Nonetheless, if despair does not consume us, we will always be lured toward the next failed promise of happiness. And each dissatisfaction carries us one step closer to death.

Pascal thinks that real happiness can be found in the quiet of our own rooms. It does not require that we win wars, engage in new trade, or discover new variants among beetles. If we cannot find satisfaction quietly in our own home, this is not because a quiet home interrupts happiness (168). Quiet is the backdrop against which happiness, or its absence, is revealed with the fewest distractions. If true happiness is present, it will be present in a quiet room. If it is not present, the fidgeting will begin. In a bland room, our emptiness is exposed. Our wretchedness is unresponsive to consolation and can be endured only by being ignored. We can only ignore it if we have endless sources of distraction and diversion.

At this point, though Pascal seems morbid and dark, he insists that if we are going to find a therapy that fits our true circumstance, we must have a thorough assessment and diagnosis. We run in terror from Pascal's three questions. The only way for him to break the power that distraction has on us is to blare his warning until we turn off the television, disconnect the video games, place the self-help and dieting books back on the shelf, and turn the conversation toward consideration of the hardest of the three questions: "What should I do now?" Given our relatively benighted state, we can only trudge toward an answer. We must reason tediously from principles instead of grasping the truth with a glance (622). Pascal was a master of mathematical and scientific thinking, but he knew that understanding mathematical or causally determined relationships in the natural world can never lead to the answers for the central questions about our condition. If those are our only resources, everything is just an investigation of the details of our despair. Studying the human condition requires the philosophical subjects. But Pascal knew that far fewer people pursue philosophy than mathematics or science (566). Waking people to their true condition is difficult.

As with everything else, our search for moral knowledge neither starts nor ends with certainty. "The harbor judges those on board ship. But where will we find a harbor in morals?" (576). Galileo and Einstein showed us why the harbor cannot judge those on board ship any more legitimately than those on board ship can judge the harbor. There are no fixed points in our exploration of the natural and the moral world. Part of why we drift in the domain of morality is that we are missing the answer to an important question: What is the meaning of death for us? The answer is as important as it is uncertain. Pascal writes, "There can be no doubt that whether the soul is mortal or immortal ought to make the whole difference in ethics. And yet philosophers have drawn up their ethics independently of this!" (505). The tension between urgency and uncertainty is our refrain.

No matter what the relevance of immortality or mortality might be to a philosopher's draft of an ethics, my fate after death seems at least interesting. But for Pascal, the question is not merely interesting: "Nothing is so important to a man as his condition. Nothing is so frightening to him as eternity" (681). We fret and become agitated if we are passed over for a promotion, get a ding in the door of our new car, or sense that our neighbor is gossiping about us behind our backs. But we rarely mention the enormous fact that we are going to die and that when we do we lose *everything*. Even if we do acknowledge mortality by purchasing life insurance, or going to the funeral of a relative or a friend, we still quickly return to wringing our hands over declines in the stock market. Our thoughts about eternity are transient. This is so odd. Why do we ignore this massive fact about our existence? "It is an incomprehensible spell, a supernatural sloth, which points to an all-powerful force as its cause" (281). This apparent sloth is common, but people who seem uninterested in what happens at death might be pretending. For Pascal, people who are actually satisfied with viewing themselves as a transient vapor, and who feel no terror at this state of things, should be pitied—it is the saddest thing in the world.

Is Pascal right? Does it have to be sad? Apparently not. Many people think that this transient and ultimately meaningless awakening of the universe to itself in the form of our conscious thought and feeling is enough. The tragic contrast between the magnitude of the event of our consciousness and shortness of its duration is even seen as beautiful by some. The prospect of enjoying the universe for a time and then disappearing forever can be comforting. To this Pascal has little left to say except to ask, "What if there *is* more?" What if satisfaction with being a transient, conscious vapor is to settle for one good, but to miss the possibility of a life that could be incomparably more satisfying if there actually were a God? Would it make a difference to you if the conscious experience of beauty, goodness, and purpose in the universe revealed a creator? Would it matter to you if longing, love, and the search for meaning could be met with something as ultimately fulfilling as God? Even if someone says, "There is no God, so I must find satisfaction elsewhere," Pascal insists that if there *were* a God we would be happier, and if a God *would* make us happier in the truest sense, then we are creatures who in some manner are made for God, even as we are made for water and find that it quenches our thirst, made for bread and find that it satisfies our hunger (18). He wants to shake us into honesty about what *would* constitute our deepest happiness, not in order to show anything about the truth of the universe, but rather to show us something about the truth of ourselves. He wants to point to our loves and losses in order to force us to acknowledge that life as a conscious but transient accidental vapor on a speck in the vast purposeless universe, however beautiful the moment, still leaves us unsatisfied and bewildered. This is not some jaundiced and parsimonious dissatisfaction that is reasonably met with the question, "Why can't you just be satisfied with the good in your life?" Instead, it is an awareness of honest desire. It is a willingness to ask why humanity ever desired God in the first place. It is a refusal to allow ourselves to settle for less than what our inner urge insists *ought* to be the case. We must seek the whole truth with the same urgency a parent might seek out a child, thought to be lost forever, when some strange clue suggests that things might be otherwise. A parent like that will never rest and will be thinking about the child even as they do other things in the day. We do not have to know what God is. Pascal, like Thomas Aquinas, did not know. This frees us to respond to our inkling that there is more to beauty, more to truth, more to meaning, and more to our longing for something-we-know-not-what beyond death. We can even call out for "God" in the middle of this strange circumstance, without having to force ourselves to believe in an impossible picture of God. This frees us to pray one of the most important prayers a person can pray: "Are You there?" (680). This prayer is nothing more than a willed openness to the possibility of encountering God as a person, in light of true desire. Such openness (or the refusal of such openness) *defines* philosophical style because everything from science, to beauty, to love, to death is altered when viewed through one lens, *there is a God*, or another, *there is no God*.

Where are we? What kind of universe do we live in? What is the nature of the eternity on either side of my earthly sojourn? We do not know. Pascal prods us toward disturbance and agitation in the face of this uncertainty. Tranquility that follows from a lack of interest in these questions is a monstrous waste. "We must make those who spend their lives in this way feel the outrageousness and stupidity of it by pointing it out to them, so that they are overcome by the recognition of their folly" (682). Of course, if all were darkness with absolutely nothing suggesting the possibility that there is a God, it would be easy. Or if all were light with clear and undeniable signs of God everywhere we look, it would be easy. But that is not our state. We are awake, aware, and certain to die. "In the state in which I am, not knowing what I am or what I ought to do, I know neither my condition nor my duty. My whole heart longs to know where the true good lies in order to follow it" (682). Only when we are at this point are we ready to ask the third question in our search for a philosophical style that frames the meanings and guides the actions that fill our life: What should I do now?

What Should I Do Now?

After hearing Pascal's account of who we are and where we are, the beginning of his answer to the third question is not terribly surprising. "I blame equally those who decide to praise man, those who blame him, and those who want to be diverted. I can only approve those who search in anguish" (24). No wonder that he uses the metaphor of a prisoner in a prison cell to explain his position. If I am waiting for a judge to say whether I will be condemned to life in prison or be restored to freedom, it would be very strange if I didn't care about the deliberations and instead just wanted to sit in my cell doing Sudoku puzzles (195). But I might say, "I will find out one way or the other, so why pay attention?" Fine, we can change the story. Suppose the judge took into account your interest in your fate as she came to a decision. If you care about the decision, you are worthy of freedom. If you don't care enough about freedom to even inquire, then you are not worthy of freedom. But that change in the metaphor is not very compelling.

So, what about this: "Freedom is yours for the taking. You will not be forced to inquire, nor to take the freedom, nor to gather your things, nor to walk out the door. If you care so little about your freedom that you are content to sit in jail playing Sudoku puzzles, so much the worse for you. But why would you not want to taste freedom now? Even if your freedom will not be granted, what do you lose by asking?" If we want to save the metaphor, that might be a bit more satisfying. These revisions fit the usual characterization of Pascal's arguments, in which calculation of benefit to oneself is at the center. But I think this way of viewing Pascal's project does not do justice to the arguments, nor to Pascal. Calculations of benefit function as the mechanics that start the inquiry. These mechanics finally depend not on rational assessment of risk and possibility, but rather on our proclivity for gambling and our hope that something meaningful will be discovered in our anxious struggle to grasp the truth of our short lives. The arguments start with something rather base, something that is no better than any other self-serving and diverting gamble. But in the end, this part of the argument is distilled into a blunt challenge: if you are going to play gambling games, let's at least play the game with the highest stakes.

Go back to the prison cell metaphor. Pascal just wants us to be honest about our surprise. The prisoner will either get life in prison, or be released from the dank and lonely cell. If a person does not care about the outcome, something is deeply wrong: if we do not feel the urgency attached to fate, provoking the quest for wisdom, there is something wrong with us. We should be distressed. The wager Pascal proposes does have an element of calculation, but it is intended to get us off the couch and out of our apathy. He wants to start us on our anguished search. His bet is that once we start on the search, we will find something important, something we can only find by engaging in the search, however full of doubt and uncertainty we are when we start. If crassness and vulgarity get us moving, Pascal will be crass and vulgar.

We will resist. When we do, he will point out that plunging ahead despite uncertainty is part of our daily life anytime we board a plane, engage in war, or marry. Therefore, when uncertainty looms over questions of universal significance, we should not let it distract us (480). Our lives would be profoundly impoverished if they were limited to what is certain. The need for certainty is paralyzing. Everything we see is uncertain and unstable. "So let us not look for certainty and stability" (230).

We have several options. We can foster the illusion that certainty is attainable. If we do this, we will refuse philosophical styles that embrace uncertainty. But this just *is* to choose a philosophical style without certainty that we are right. We can also try to avoid questions about the meaning of our lives and attach ourselves to a few things that distract us for roughly seventy to eighty years—getting the house paid off, achieving a promotion, finally buying that boat. But this too is a commitment to a philosophical style that answers life's questions in a very particular way.

Any commitment to a philosophical style is also an act of faith. Once we see this, we can open ourselves to the possibility that there is more to the universe than we might imagine. This is an invitation to an adventure that enlivened Pascal: "I have sought to find whether this God has not left some mark of himself" (229). Pascal is uninterested in trying to prove the existence of God. He invented probability theory by working on games of chance, and the most important game of chance is the game we call "living." This is where he raises his strange question: Is it probable that probability brings certainty? His answer is a resounding *yes*. If it is even *possible* that there is more to reality than the accidental, purposeless eruption of the universe, and if it even *might* be the case that this possible "more" includes the existence of God, then it approaches *certainty* that this possibility should be at the heart of my own philosophical style as I answer the question, "What should I do?" Our only certainty is that our quest ought to include, or even be devoted to, searching for this possible God, and living as though God exists, because if God is more like a person than a rock or a mathematical formula, living this way might well be the condition for discovery (496).

Pascal knows that this is easier said than done. Sometimes he provokes us by offering a crass calculation of risk and benefit. He prods us by saying that even if the universe is an accidental, purposeless conglomeration of atoms in the void, the net gain in a life spent searching for God *still* makes that choice most reasonable. He also recognizes that there are motives for refusing to do this, despite his arguments from probability. After all, in the middle of our misery and suffering, our games, cars, and pleasure-responsive bodies console us, however temporarily. But this only deepens the wretchedness of our lives. These diversions relieve our boredom, but boredom is the very thing that might compel us to find better answers (33). Relief from boredom undermines our chances of finding the most valuable thing in our lives.

Be honest, he says. There are things that feel natural to us, not in the sense that swallowing, breathing, and sleeping are natural to us, but in the sense of seeming right—telling the truth mostly, not killing people mostly, not stealing mostly. Yes, if there is a creator, these things might be obligatory in a different way, and to different effect, than they would be without a creator. But even apart from faith or revelation, those who oppose lying, killing people, and stealing (all things considered) do so from a feeling that is uncertain, but that nonetheless powerfully *inclines*. For most of us, moral choices somehow *feel* right. They *feel* like more than mere preferences. This does not prove anything, and the language of "feeling" does not sit well with many. Pascal is quick to acknowledge this resistance. He is also quick to reject it. "It is through the heart that we know first principles, and reason which has no part in this knowledge vainly tries to contest them" (142). If we limit ourselves to what reason can demonstrate, our efforts to understand our three questions will fail, or at least be incomplete. We cannot rely on reason only, but neither can we rely only on the "heart," nor on our abilities to have sudden insight, to feel, and to experience reality through epiphany, allusion, or faith. We must use *every* gift to see the world as truly as possible. Even wine can play a part in this quest. "If you give someone none, he cannot discover the truth. It is the same if you give him too much" (72).

To live without caring about who we are, where we are, and what we ought to do is pathetic. But it is not as bad as believing that we are created by God with a genuine purpose, and then living badly despite that belief (516). If you believe, act accordingly. If you do not believe in a God who is relevant to our search for answers, you still have many questions to answer. For example, if you are a firmly convinced ontological naturalist, how do you answer the question, "What should we do?" How do you know? Could the answer be different? Someone who believes that nothing exists except the material of a purposeless universe, and that we have shown up as a surprising and temporary anomaly, might nonetheless assert with conviction that we should be just, or perhaps that we should maximize pleasure, happiness, or the good (whatever that is). But those buckets can spring leaks when we seriously ask, "Why should I bother acting one way rather than another?"

This is the starting point from which much of Pascal's own search begins. The *heart's* convictions regarding the reality of love, purpose, and beauty are compelling enough for us to ask whether the existence of God would make those convictions more intelligible, or less. That is a good question, but Pascal knows that even scripture characterizes God as hidden. He thinks it is absurd to try to prove God's existence from what we experience in the natural world. From the perspective of faith the universe lights up as the work of a creator, and it is illuminated with the kind of mystery and suggestiveness that has inspired much of the great poetry and art that Nietzsche claimed could only be produced under the conviction that there is a

God. But if one looks at the world from the perspective of nontheism, there is nothing in nature that moves us irresistibly toward belief in God. The organization of a grasshopper or the course of the moon inspires a peculiar delight for someone who already believes in God. But if this is offered as a proof for the existence of God, the argument inspires contempt in the nontheist. It is a contempt that Pascal shared. He thought that people who offer such arguments actually weaken the more compelling arguments for religion (644). That said, it would be interesting to know what Pascal would think of the many contemporary scientists who do think that the order of nature points more to a mindlike origin rather than to an overwhelmingly improbable eruption from nothing (I am thinking here of Simon Conway Morris, Jennifer Wiseman, Freeman Dyson, John Polkinghorn, Ard Louis, John Lennox, Francis Collins, Joel Primack, Michael Polanyi, Max Planck, and Robert Millikan, to name a few of the many prominent scientists from the last seventy years of scientific progress who are theists).

So where do we start, if not with nature? The starting point we have is our own lived experience of the local universe. This experience is qualitatively different from anything catalogued and described by any science. Only from within mindful attention to lived experience can we answer the question, "What should I do now?" Pay attention. Stay open to surprise. This is the first thing we must do. What do we find when we pay attention? We quickly discover, yet again, that we do not want to be bored. To avoid boredom we will do almost anything. But every solution for boredom is reducible to the hunt, the gamble. We pursue a lover, we pursue a battle, we run for office. But we do not pursue these because we want to arrive at a settled and peaceful existence, allowing us to turn our attention to contemplation of our true condition. No. We *want* the hustle, bustle, distraction, and amusement. "We prefer the hunt to the kill" (168). Consider gambling. Suppose the stakes are modest—fifty dollars. If I say to the gambler, "I will give you fifty dollars so that you do not have to gamble," will that satisfy him? No. That would ruin his distraction and excitement, and he would be unhappy. This is not to say that gamblers (or venture capitalists, or promiscuous lovers, or politicians) deliberately deceive themselves into thinking that one more win, one more contract, or one more erotic adventure will provide the desired satisfaction. No, this deception is just part of our human character. It is built in. But if gamblers are ever disabused of this deception, they become doubly unhappy because they see the vanity of the pursuit, and yet they are compelled toward the gamble anyway, and their wretchedness is made worse.

This is a good thing from Pascal's perspective. This is where he has something to say. You want to gamble? Fine. Raise the stakes. Instead of trading on the value of a dollar or a poker chip, trade on the value of your life. Why not throw in the possibility—even though it is *only* a possibility—that the stakes are not merely high, but that they may even be eternal? This is not a trick. Pascal claims no more certainty about the existence of God than any agnostic or nontheist, at least for the purposes of articulating his starting point. There is a God, or there is not a God. Choose. You would have to leave the realm of logical possibility to disagree with the choice. But no matter how much you strain your reasoning abilities you will not be able to prove with certainty the truth of the question one way or the other. Nonetheless, you are in the game. You do not have a choice about whether or not you are in the game. Why? Because here you are, alive, spending your time, with no choice about whether or not you spend it. Consider the options (680). Suppose there is no God and you structure life in accordance with this view. When you are dead, you lose nothing. And while you were alive you had fulfilling work and relationships, ate good meals, and got laid. Suppose, on the other hand, there is no God, but you wagered that there is a God and structured your life according to this view. You also would have had fulfilling work and relationships, ate some good meals, and got laid (though you might have been constrained a bit by the misguided sense that a nonexistent creator cared about what you did with your body, the bodies of others, and the bodies of children that erupt into the world). True, you will likely have spent time praying in an empty universe. You will have joined a faith community. You probably will have accepted a false hope for some kind of life after death. But when you die, you still lose nothing, because you disappear, turn into dust. The universe just reverts to dead matter with no consciousness or memory.

Suppose, on the other hand, that there is a God, but rather than wagering on this view, you structure your life as though there is no God. Pascal is criticized for worrying over the possibility that you might face an eternity of damnation, but he worries because he is a mathematician, so even as a *possibility*, mere crass calculation makes eternal damnation compound the reasons not to wager in this way. But setting aside the notion of damnation, such a life would still be comparable to the man sitting in the prison cell, unaware of the good news that he is free to leave the prison. It is again a life in which there are ventures, pleasures, and risks. But it is life spent among possibilities for flourishing that are ignored. It is a life spent with other created beings for whom thought, love, and longing exist because of the love of God, but experiencing them as nothing more than unexpected and accidental results of biology, chemistry, and physics. It is living in a universe in which there is an inexhaustible well of purpose and meaning, but reducing these experiences to the byproduct of a nonconscious, purposeless universe. It is living in a universe where our longing for more has its only satisfying answer in God, but calling this longing an illusion, something to be explained by fears or habits grounded in the purposeless and accidental sequences of prior events. That life, Pascal wants to say with as much force as he can muster, is a *far* more unfortunate life than one spent searching for God in a universe that has no God.

The final possibility, of course, is that we live in a universe created by God, and that despite the incomprehensibility of God, it is God who provokes our longing and our search. If only God can satisfy our longing for God, we can stop pretending that something besides God can satisfy us. Along the way there will almost certainly be times when we lean toward doubt more than toward faith, but even then we can pray, "God, are you there?" We can pray this with integrity, because we know that we can be satisfied by nothing less, and nothing other, than God. We need God, and in God alone are our longings and deepest desires fully met. In this universe, however faltering our way, we can live as people of hope. And maybe that hope will be answered.

That is the wager. It is not a gimmick that is supposed to yield belief, as though we could force belief. Rather, it is a way of acknowledging what is at stake. In the face of our unavoidable uncertainty and the urgency introduced by our impending death, theists wager on a philosophical style oriented toward the possibility of God. This does not mean that we are free of doubt. But even as doubt rides sidekick on the journey, reminding us of the uncertainty that pervades our experience, we do the best we can by beginning to *live as though*, in prayer, in obedience, in conversation with friends, and in worship. Toward ourselves, toward others, and toward God, we begin by *acting as though*, which is the only gesture of faith we might be capable of when we cannot quell our seasons of doubt. We act as though our longing meaningfully points toward God rather than being an accidental byproduct of purposeless events—an *allusion* rather than an *illusion*. Pascal does not like the discomfort of our current state, but it cannot be any other way. This does not mean living without a robust mirth—far from it. It is actually an invitation, in the face of uncertainty, to live joyfully in the local universe, complete with all its beauty and all its suffering. If you have ever hesitated to get on a roller coaster, worrying over what is ahead, but finally buckled yourself in, then you know the feeling that there is no way to do anything but ride the ride to the end. We are all most assuredly and irrevocably strapped in. There is no way off the ride except to ride it to the end. But this very necessity can itself relieve our fretting. Wringing your hands will do no good.

The wager requires real *engagement*. This can occur in many forms. From within his own experience of living in this way, Pascal discovered that these commitments transform our vision of beauty, suffering, and being in the world. With practice we can learn to see aspects of reality that we could not otherwise have seen. Acting *as though* is not the last act in the wager.

The end of the wager—both in the sense of its goal and in the sense of the argument coming to an end—is a challenge to live in a certain way, and then to ask whether this approach opens up the truth of the world, or else deranges the truth of the world. It is not an invitation to force belief. Neither is it an argument to feel a certain way. The whole thing is summed up in that prayer that anyone can pray with integrity because it does not require us to believe or feel in any particular way: "Are you there?" The answer may be yes. The answer may be no. The prayer is best prayed without a preset form that the answer must take. The answer may not come in a form that can be expressed as a proposition or as an argument, which is what Pascal means when he says that the heart has reasons of its own that reason does not know. The answer may not be a one-time yes or no. The habit of praying "Are you there?" is a habit of openness to the possibility of God. Mere openness to the possibility of God may itself be a condition for seeing what is real about the world. There is nothing surprising about this. So much of what we learn about the world requires openness to what we do not know. This is the premise of any real effort to teach. A student must, in a sense, proceed on trust that there is a real world to discover in, say, mathematics, music, or the identification of wines from different regions.

Anyone who has spent time learning to read poetry knows that the first reading of a poem does not yield all of the subtleties of meaning or structure. These come only with persistent attention, often at the behest of a trusted teacher who says that the journey is worth it. In our first encounter with Mozart's G-minor Symphony, and in our tenth, the same notes are played. Everything is there musically in both settings, but during the tenth performance we are able to hear things that we were not able to hear during the first. With the experiences of God, should there turn out to be a God, it may well be the same. It may well be, for example, that the witness of the saints reminds of something to which we have grown dull. This is the real wager: live so that you learn to hear, just in case there is anything to hear. If there is nothing to hear, when you die nothing is lost. But if there is something to hear, there will be incalculable gain.

This potential gain (and potential loss) on this side of death can be framed by a second question that is thought or prayed. The first question was, "Are you there?" The second question is, "What if you are there?" The first question creates a kind of focused openness to possibility. If the saints are even *possibly* credible, their experience provides evidence of divine presence, love, or something harder to name. This evidence can be dismissed. But there is no definitive counterevidence, so if it is dismissed, it is dismissed based on an assumed worldview. No functional MRI of the brains of saints experiencing God has any relevance to the veracity of the saints' claims, just as no fMRI of Einstein's brain that lit up in a certain area while he was demonstrating his theory of general relativity would count as evidence for or against the truth of general relativity.

Over a lifetime, anyone who asks the first question has a possible adventure ahead as they learn how to use the second question in the way that they might use a candle to find their way in the dark. This second question is meant to illuminate, and it requires some persistence, because it is both a tool and a habit. It takes practice.

"Why should I bother?" That is a fair question. The answer is that you will develop a habit of seeing, one way or the other. You cannot escape. You must embrace a habit of some sort. Along the way, pay attention to the consequences of your habit. Imagine a parent looking at the child she loves. She can follow Bertrand Russell and learn to see the world like he did. Russell said that though we call ourselves persons and seem to see each other this way, we are in fact no more than physical mechanisms whose thoughts and bodily movements "follow the same laws that describe the motions of stars and atoms."[2] This collapses the distinction between persons and things. What about our ability to think? "What we call our 'thoughts' seem to depend upon the organization of tracks in the brain in the same sort of way in which journeys depend upon roads and railways. The energy used in

2. Russell, "What I Believe," in *Why I Am Not a Christian*, 50.

thinking seems to have a chemical origin."[3] The fact that roads and railways are deliberately constructed, with a distinct purpose and goal, is not likely an extension of the metaphor that Russell would approve. His perspective was derived from the early exploration of neurophysiology, and the details of the brain's stochastic chemistry can be further elaborated endlessly. But finally, however appearance shows up, Pascal's question is about our actual *experience* of the world. The parent who sees her child can say, "I *feel* love for you, but I *know* you are chemistry, with the same status in the universe as any beaker of saltwater or mud puddle." This deepens the habit of seeing in a certain way. Despite her uncertainty, this is an understanding of the world as she has so far encountered it. This is one kind of fallible philosophical style that she might embrace. Even if her worldview was given to her by her own parents, she must choose whether or not to consolidate the habit of seeing the world this way, given her lived experience.

Another way to understand her experience of her child is to ask the second question, "What if God is there?" Does that change her thoughts about her child? Does the child's apparent personhood and presence seem obscured, or does its reality seem clarified? Again, the purpose of the two questions is not to prove God's existence. Pascal, along with many of us, would say that God's existence can be neither proved nor disproved. Asking the two questions is a way of meaningfully living out the wager over the course of a life. We risk, we observe, and we pay attention to how experience is illuminated or diminished along the way.

We can take the same approach to friendship. The ontological naturalist must explain friendship and the delight we take in conversations about our projects, fears, hopes, and our sense of meaning in the world. Friendship may be a way of winning security in a hostile world. Perhaps groups capable of friendship have other characteristics that increase their likelihood of faring well in the world—a stronger inclination, for example, to cooperate in community projects that are too big for one individual, projects such as food production or battle with tribal enemies. That is one way to wager, deepening a habit of seeing the world until it is hard to imagine the world being any other way. But, given how little we know, we might wager differently. In the context of friendship, we might ask, "What if God is there?" What impact would that have on the meaning and value of friendship? Would the reality of friendship, and our value of it, make more sense in a world with a God, or in a naturalist's world? This is the

3. Ibid.

moment-by-moment exercise of the wager. It is a habit, a repeated act, not a one-time event. This is why philosophical style develops over a lifetime.

Either we frame the meaning of our lives as though there is a God, or we frame the meaning as though there is not a God. This does not mean that we actually behave as though we were only accidental collections of purposeless atoms. We generally behave as though this is not the case. Our behavior mostly looks like what we would expect from creatures who are much more than accidental collections of purposeless atoms. The wager is about how we orient ourselves toward the world that we actually experience. We listen to music. Bach's concertos cannot compel us toward a definitive conclusion about their origin, meaning, and purpose. We bring our philosophical style to the experience. If we begin in the ontological naturalist's universe, we will have theories and explanations that offer an account for Bach's brain, and our own, and our theory will be, roughly, that creating Bach's music and then listening to it is an interesting manifestation of neurochemical reactions that are, as chemical reactions go, qualitatively no different than the chemical reaction in a beaker when a teaspoon of sugar dissolves in water. On the other hand, with the now-familiar pattern, if we have wagered differently we might ask, "What if God is there?" We listen to a Bach concerto. What is the effect of this alternate view on our experience of the music? Is there any way in which the music makes more sense if there is a God? Is there any way in which it makes less sense?

Of course this could go on and on with our experience of poetry, wine, flowers, laughter, and the companionship of animals with faces. It might illuminate our experience of joy, wonder, and natural beauty. How are such experiences impacted when we orient ourselves using the question, "What if God is there?" When we protest injustice, bemoan the greed of nations that leads to the starvation of so many, rage against the Holocaust, or insist that our children tell the truth in most circumstances, do these intuitions carry different weights when framed by an accidental and purposeless universe, compared to being framed by a universe created by God? If we live the wager in the direction of the questions "Are you there?" and "What if you are there?" does this illuminate our moral discourse, reasoning, and feeling, or do our moral activities make less sense?

Our view of science is also affected by our wager one way or the other. When we approach the meaning of the data mined through biology, will we do so as Francis Crick, who is an atheist, or as Simon Conway Morris, who is a Christian? When we study the data and theories of physics, and consider how these relate to the rest of our knowledge and experience, will we do so from the starting point of Stephen Hawking (who is sort of an atheist), that of Albert Einstein (who got upset when people called him an atheist), or that of George Lemaître (the theoretical physicist who proposed the Big Bang theory, and who was also a Catholic priest)? The effect of various wagers on our sense of the meaning of what we discover in the physical universe would take a book of its own—a very long book. The point is this: when we orient ourselves using the second question, "What if God is there?" we are only asking whether or not the existence of God would illuminate the fact that we have minds. Our minds can explore and grasp the strange complexity of the natural world, the moral world, and the world of beauty. Would the existence of God make the reality of our rational minds more surprising, or less surprising, than if they have erupted in an accidental and purposeless universe? Clearly, living the wager in this way is not a simple or simplistic approach to spending our few years on this earth. The complexities of our diverse responses are worthy of mature and respectful attention as we each grow toward the best conclusions we can, variably fretting and rejoicing along the way.

Suffering and evil are also important aspects of our experience of wagering. Children die of cancers in one decade, though they might have been saved in the next. The difference between the two decades is nothing more than the progress of medical science achieved by our minds and our industry. In the absence of God this is not surprising. What if we ask our two questions, "Are you there?" and "What if you are there?" One fitting response is to ask another question: "Why, if you *are* there, do you allow the suffering and loss to continue?" Whatever our answer might be, it will include the uncertainty of our wagers in an important and serious sense. But the wager is not a propositional exercise that we can do in our heads, abstractly. The wager is *lived*. To ask the questions from within the experience of suffering requires that we experience the suffering in some way, just as we must have experienced love, joy, beauty, and music in order for our questions to be truly illuminating. The wager is not a circumscribed arena for debate about why, if there *is* a God, children's arms are cut off in Rwanda, pregnant women are crushed in the rubble after an earthquake in Haiti, or tens of thousands die in a tsunami in Indonesia. No. From within the *lived experience* of suffering, the wager is likewise *lived*. As I lay on my deathbed struggling for breath, I pray, "Are you there?" and "What if you are there?" The rest is not writable because it can only be lived. If my children starve while food sent from other nations rots in the harbor because of unjust circumstances and a corrupt government misusing its power in order to prevent distribution, from *within* that experience I can pray the two questions as part of the life I have wagered. The wager does not anticipate the answer. The answer is not spoken or written. The answer can only be *lived*. The wager does, of course, require openness to answers that may be surprising. Pascal was a Christian. At the center of his faith was the image of Jesus dying on a cross at the hands of the Roman army after asking God to let this cup pass, and crying out from the cross, "My God, my God, why have you forsaken me?" That worldview does not have simple, comfortable, formulaic responses to the experiences of suffering and prayerful lament.

The wager must be lived from within experience. One experience is that of suffering. Another experience is the sense that things *ought* to be otherwise. I will not press too hard on the word *experience*. But I intend the word to contrast with conclusions drawn from thought about suffering in the abstract. I am not talking about an *argument* that things should be otherwise. I am talking about our *experience* that things ought to be otherwise. This experience compelled Pascal to say that the heart knows things that reason cannot grasp. We witness greed and selfishness that impoverish whole nations, leading to hunger in the middle of abundance. We witness rape, child abuse, and slavery. We witness genocide, torture, and the malevolent use of the pain-sensitive bodies of animals for ignoble purposes. And we want to cry out that this is wrong, not merely in the sense that we prefer pleasure to pain, but in a deeper sense. When we feel outrage at injustice and abuse, and when we sense that things *ought* to be otherwise, the wager leads us back to the question, "What if God is there?" This is not a question of theodicy. It is a question of whether or not our *sense* that there is a way things *ought* to be is illuminated more by the existence of God than by the nonexistence of God. Within an accidental, purposeless universe erupting from nothing, there is no way things "ought" to be. You can only say that things ought to be otherwise, if there actually *is* a way things ought to be. But you can only say there is a way things ought to be if someone intended the universe to be a certain way. The work of theodicy, for those who think it is worthwhile, is motivated by the intuition that our conviction that *things ought to be otherwise* makes more sense if there is a God, even though we do not grasp why things are *not* as they ought to be. In any case the wager is not about a set of propositions that constitute a theodicy. It is about living our lives one way or another.

We cannot say how a life wagered in this way will be experienced. We cannot say what, or who, will be discovered in the course of such a life. But life will never outlast the reasonableness of pursuing the wager that God is with us, even if the wager only takes the form of praying our two questions, "Are you there?" and "What if you are there?" Pascal's hyperbole went too far when he said, "There are only three kinds of people: those who serve God having found him; others who spend their time seeking him who have not found him; and the rest who live without seeking him nor having found him. The first are reasonable and happy, the last are lunatic and unhappy, those in the middle are unhappy and reasonable" (192). Lunacy has often enough led to the appearance of a bizarre, and sometime hurtful, faith of sorts. Sorrow has often enough led to a life in which the possibilities opened by the wager simply fall flat and dull, where even the *possibility* of God seems to illuminate nothing. But many people who spend their time on this adventure, myself included, find the world lighting up and even small experiences being transformed. These can live life most fully as a gift because there is someone to thank. In the end, philosophical style comes down to this: wager, and then live. But do it now, because now is all you have.

Bibliography

Aquinas, Thomas. *Summa Theologica*. Translated by Fathers of the English Dominican Province. 5 vols. Westminster, MD: Christian Classics, 1948.

Aristotle. *The Complete Works of Aristotle: The Revised Oxford Translation*. Edited by Jonathan Barnes. 2 vols. Princeton: Princeton University Press, 1984.

Balthasar, Hans Urs von. *The Glory of the Lord: A Theological Aesthetics*. Vol. 2, *Studies in Theological Style: Clerical Styles*. Translated by Andrew Louth et al. San Francisco: Ignatius Press, 1984.

Chamisso, Adelbert von. *Peter Schlemihl, the Shadowless Man*. Translated by Sarah Austin. London: Cassell, 2012 (adapted).

Frost, Robert. "Design." Online: https://www.poets.org/poetsorg/poem/design.

Galilei, Galileo. *Sidereus Nuncius, or The Sidereal Messenger*. Translated by Albert van Helden. Chicago: University of Chicago Press, 1989.

Gilson, Etienne. *Being and Some Philosophers*. 2nd ed. Toronto: Pontifical Institute of Mediaeval Studies, 1952.

Le Guin, Ursala K. *The Wind's Twelve Quarters: Stories*. New York: HarperCollins, 2004.

Pascal, Blaise. *Pensées and Other Writings*. Translated by Honor Levi. Edited by Anthony Levi. Oxford: Oxford University Press, 2008.

Rosenberg, Alex. *An Atheist's Guide to Reality: Enjoying Life without Illusions*. New York: Norton, 2012.

Russell, Bertrand. *Why I Am Not a Christian, and Other Essays on Religion and Related Subjects*. Edited by Paul Edwards. New York: Simon and Schuster, 1957.

Scarry, Elaine. *The Body in Pain: The Making and Unmaking of a World*. New York: Oxford University Press, 1985.

Made in the USA
San Bernardino, CA
11 April 2019